THE ULTIMATE
KITE BOOK

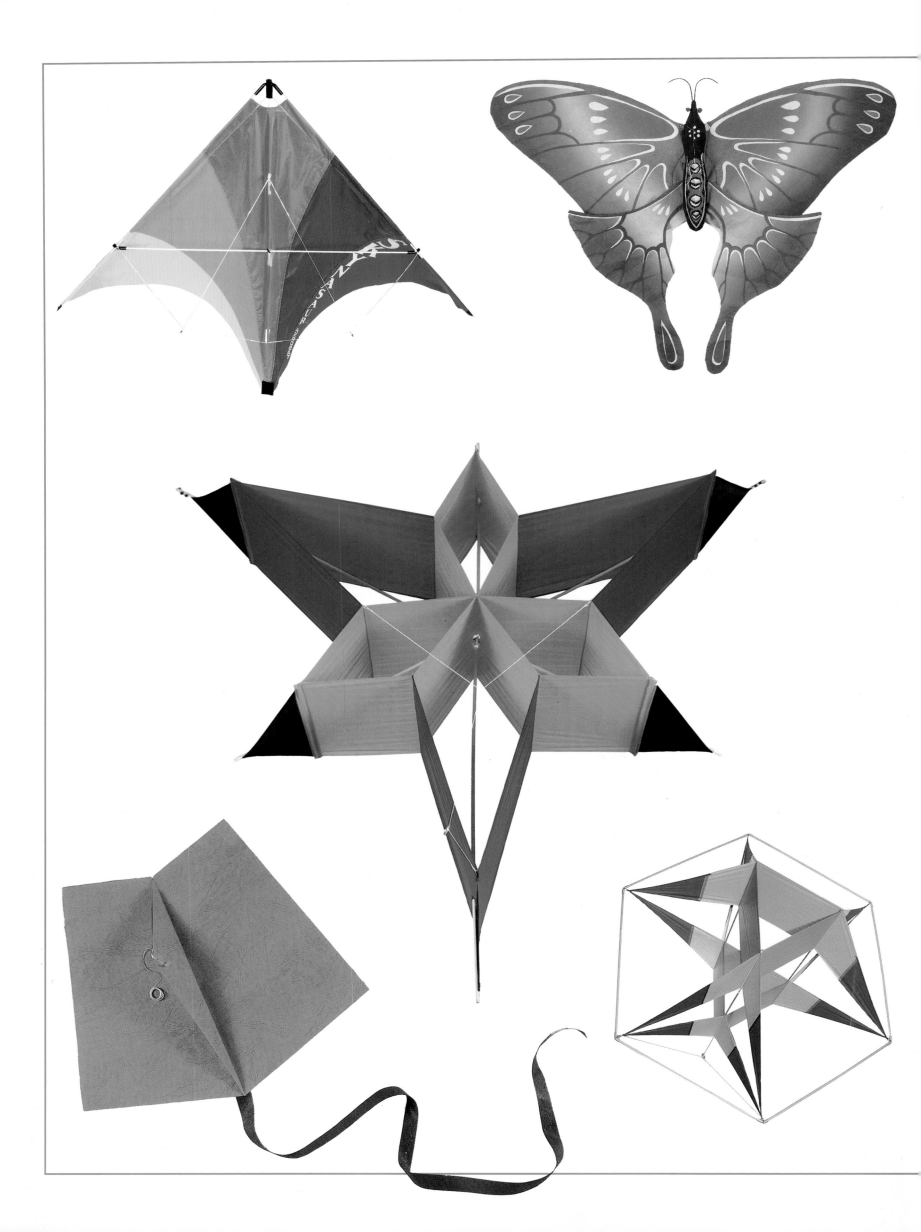

THE ULTIMATE
KITE BOOK

PAUL & HELENE MORGAN

SIMON AND SCHUSTER

New York London Toronto Sydney Tokyo Singapore

A DORLING KINDERSLEY BOOK

SIMON AND SCHUSTER

Simon & Schuster Building
Rockefeller Center
1230 Avenue of the Americas
New York, New York 10020

Project editor
Tanya Hines

Design
Nigel Osborne Associates

Senior managing editor
Daphne Razazan

Managing art editor
Carole Ash

Production
Helen Creeke

Reproduced in Singapore by Colourscan
Printed and bound in Italy by New Interlitho

10 9 8 7 6 5 4 3 2 1
Library of Congress Cataloguing-in-Publication Data

Morgan, Paul, 1956-
    The ultimate kite book / Paul and Helene Morgan.
        p. cm.
    Includes index.
    ISBN: 0-671-74443-7
    1. Kites I. Morgan, Helene. II. Title.
TL759.M66 1992
629. 133'32--dc20   91-33506
                                         CIP

CONTENTS

INTRODUCTION

With an ever-increasing number of kites on the market, from simple flat and bowed kites to geometric aerial sculptures and high-tech stunters, kite-flying is entering a new era of popularity. The perfect 'green' hobby, it can be practiced by anyone, young or old, in an urban park or an open meadow.

Kite-flying opens up a variety of experiences. The very young love the excitement of flying a small kite for the first time, and seeing it dart around in the wind, with its tail making shapes in the sky. For the older flyer, watching a large, heavy box kite flying overhead in almost total silence can be very relaxing and peaceful. In contrast, controlling a stunter in a complex series of maneuvers can provide an exhilarating challenge as the flyer tries to match his skills against the wind.

We became involved in kite-flying through buying a plastic octopus kite at the beach for our young son Jonathan. The kite stayed up all day and we were reluctant to bring it down. The next day, we bought another kite, of a slightly different design. From then on, we were hooked. We found as many books as we could about the subject and, following the patterns in the books, began to make our first kites. The instructions were not always clear, so initially we made mistakes, but we soon got a lot of pleasure out of successfully making and flying our own kites. Becoming more adventurous, we altered the patterns to see how this affected the way that the kites flew. Before long, we were seeing potential kite shapes in everything, and had created several kites that we had taken through from initial concept to finished kite.

At this time, we decided that the hobby might just pay for itself, so with the encouragement of the local kite group, we approached a bank and in 1986 started in business as Morgan Kites. At first, we made a small range of kites: some our exclusive designs, others classics, but since then, we have gone from strength to strength and now sell our kites worldwide. We have included patterns for some of our own designs in the book.

Our most recent venture has been to set up a shop of our own, called Sky Bums, where we sell kites from many different countries, as well as specializing in our own high-quality, high-performance kites. We still derive the same thrills and enjoyment from making kites as in the early days, especially when we create one-off designs or special kites. We hope that your enthusiasm for kites and kite-flying will be fired from reading this book: it is always extremely satisfying to win over new converts to kiting.

Paul Morgan

Helene Morgan

A HISTORY OF KITES

The fascinating story of kites begins in the Far East, where they were first flown some two and a half thousand years ago. The earliest kites were often bird shaped and came to be steeped in symbolic significance. This tradition persists today in the Orient, where kites still play a central role in local folklore and legend. Kites spread to the West as trade proliferated during the Age of Discovery. Gradually their power as a flying instrument was recognized and exploited, reaching a crescendo of innovative uses in the nineteenth century.

KITES IN THE EAST

Although the precise origins of kites are lost in legend, the first recorded reference comes from China in about 500 BC, when a craftsman built what was probably a wooden bird kite. The early Chinese kites were magnificent constructions of silk and bamboo, but with the introduction of cheap paper around the second century AD, the kite became more widely available; many festivals and games based on kite-flying were born.

Traditional Chinese kites
Highly decorative kites have been flown for centuries in China and have great symbolic significance.

Japanese New Year
A lively New Year's Day street scene in Tokyo, where the exuberance of traditional dress is matched by the ornate paper kites being flown. Mount Fuji is in the background.

Military exploits

In China and Japan, the military were quick to recognize the potential of kite-power, and many of the earliest references to kites concern their military uses. Around 200 BC, a Chinese general is credited with using a kite to estimate the distance between his forces and the walls of an enemy castle, so that he could construct a tunnel of the correct length.

At about the same time, another general attached humming devices to kites, which were then flown over his enemies at night, making them think that they were being attacked by evil spirits. Ancient Japanese prints show large kites carrying archers who fired down on their enemies.

Festivals and traditions

Throughout the Far East, kite-flying has a long association with religious practice. It formed a central role in many fertility rites and ceremonies to celebrate the birth of a child, as well as festivals to invoke benign weather or rich harvests. Ancient religious writings from India relate stories of gods and goddesses taking part in kite-fighting contests. In Indonesia, kites were regarded as messengers of the gods, and were believed to represent the soul of the person who flew them.

From China, the kite was probably taken to Korea and Japan by Buddhist missionaries. At the beginning of each year, Korean families inscribe kites with the names and birthdates of all their male children, then fly the kites and release them in the belief that they take with them any evil spirits that might have plagued the children. To pick up such a kite is to take on these evil spirits.

Traditional Japanese kites are decorated with legendary characters or good luck symbols such as the dragon, which symbolizes prosperity, or the crane or tortoise, which represents long life. On the fifth day of the fifth month, Japanese families celebrate the birth of any sons during the past year by flying brightly colored wind-inflated tubes, or windsocks, in the shape of fish.

Thailand, too, has a great tradition of flying and fighting kites. The two traditional designs are the male Chula, a large star-shaped kite, and the female Pakpao, which is a smaller diamond-shaped kite. They are flown during the monsoon to blow the rains away, and at other times of the year are used in fighting competitions, where teams of men try to entangle the kites of their opponents. Fighting kites are also popular in India, where huge crowds regularly converge for massive contests.

KITES IN THE WEST

In Europe, windsocks had been flown since Roman times, and these were possibly the forerunner of kites. Kites themselves may well have been introduced to the West in the fifteenth and sixteenth centuries by Dutch, Portuguese and English merchants trading in Far Eastern countries.

Among the earliest records of kites in Europe is a description, dated 1589, by a man named della Porta, of a rectangular kite from China, which he suggested could be used for lifting lanterns, fireworks, or even animals.

By the early eighteenth century, kites were widespread in Europe, but were seen mainly as a children's toy. Kite-fighting became an obsession in France, though, and in 1736 the sport was banned because of riot and crop damage.

The kite as a research tool
Towards the mid-eighteenth century, people began exploring the possibilities opened up by the ability to control an object in flight. Two Scotsmen, Thomas Melvill and Alexander Wilson, conducted an experiment to measure temperature variations at different altitudes. They flew six kites, with thermometers attached, in a train to a height of 3,000 ft (900 m).

Perhaps the most famous, and foolhardy, piece of research was that by Benjamin Franklin in 1752, who set out to prove that lightning was the same as generated electricity and not the wrath of God, and lofted a kite in a storm.

Pulling power
It had long been noted that a kite, once stable in flight, generated a strong pull on the line. This property was exploited to greater effect during the last century. In 1826 an Englishman, George Pocock, patented a design to use two or more large kites to pull a lightweight carriage, the *char-volant,* or flying chariot.

Others took up the idea, and by the end of the century, kites had been used for a number of different tasks, from pulling torpedoes on to their targets to drawing a cable across a gorge on the Niagara River.

Kites and electricity
Benjamin Franklin, conducting an experiment to prove the electrical nature of lightning. As the kite became wet, it conducted electricity down the line to a key. Franklin held the line by a ribbon and when he moved his knuckles towards the key, noted electrical discharges.

Man-lifting kites
The West's obsession with manned flight drew people to experiment with kites. Investigators were winched up on the kite line, using large, stable kites to provide the lift. American S.F. Cody is perhaps the name best associated with man-lifting kites (see right).

From kite to glider
In 1804, Sir George Cayley built a model glider that incorporated a kite as its main wing. He went on to build a glider that flew his coachman across a valley - the first recorded glider flight. At the end of the century, a German, Otto Lilienthal, built a kite with a wing shape like a bird's. Another pioneer, Octave Chanute, developed Lilienthal's work and designed a biplane hang-glider which helped in the experiments of the Wright brothers in America. They constructed biplane kites and larger gliders, leading to the development of the first airplane in December 1903.

High-tech kites
Around the turn of the century, kite design was rushing forwards. In 1893, an English emigrant in Australia, Lawrence Hargrave, perfected his two-celled box kite, used in weather forecasting. He also developed a soaring kite with a curved wing section for greater lift. American William Eddy was another major contributor to kite development. He invented his now famous bowed kite, stable in flight without a tail.

Kites were used for military observation and target practice and continued in this role even after the invention of aircraft. During the Second World War, kites were used to protect shipping.

After the war came another surge in development with the invention of non-rigid kites that relied on the wind for shape. Among these flexible kites was the sled, designed by William Allison in America.

In 1963, American Domina Jalbert hit upon the idea of the Parafoil kite based on an airplane wing section. A few years later, the highly maneuverable Flexifoil was invented, and soon after that, Peter Powell's stunt kite came on to the market, heralding the beginning of a new era of popular interest in kite-flying.

Saved by a kite

At the end of the last century, a Frenchman, C. Jobert, devised a system for rescuing shipwrecked sailors. Taking advantage of strong winds that tended to accompany shipping disasters, he would fly a kite with a rope attached that could be reached by those on ship, who were then winched to safety.

S.F. Cody being lofted by his famous winged box kite.

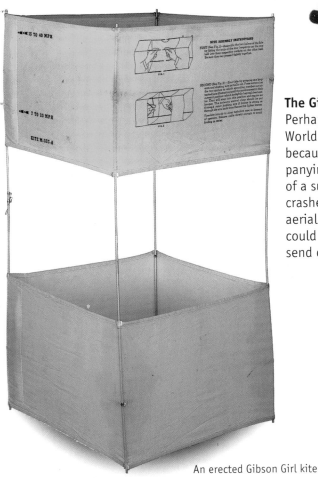

An erected Gibson Girl kite

FLAMBOYANT CODY

One of the most colorful of kiting pioneers is surely Samuel Franklin Cody, an American who settled in England. In 1901, he patented a winged version of a double-celled box kite, which was used for man-lifting. Other exploits included a kite-powered crossing of the English Channel. Despite his keenness to put his inventions to practical use, he was not taken seriously by the military: his long hair and Wild West show made him too unconventional. However, in 1906, he was given officer status at Farnborough, England, where he built the Cody war kites. He was also the first man in Britain to fly an airplane. He met his death in 1913 when another of his creations broke up in flight.

The Gibson Girl

Perhaps the most famous kite of the Second World War, the Gibson Girl was so-called because of the waist-like shape of its accompanying radio transmitter. The kite was part of a survival kit for airmen whose plane had crashed into the sea, and was flown on a thin aerial, attached to the transmitter. This could then be hand-cranked to send out an S.O.S. signal.

Curved transmitter from which the kite derives its name

Durable metal case for storing the kite

The complete survival kit

The dismantled kite

A CATALOG OF KITES

To introduce you to the enormous diversity of kite designs available today, here is a selection of classic and high-tech kites from all over the world, arranged by type of kite.

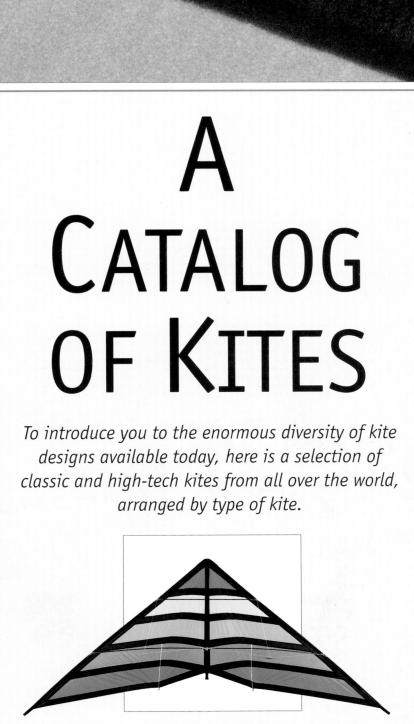

ANATOMY OF A KITE

Although kite designs vary enormously, kites have a number of basic features and components in common in terms of their framework and construction. The three kites shown below - a soft kite, a stunter and a box kite - provide a visual glossary exemplifying the key features of kite anatomy, from the leading edge to individual cells.

Jibs, small wings that allow the spars to be attached to the cover outside the main body of the kite so that tension is spread evenly throughout

SOFT KITE

With no framework to hold it rigid, a soft kite is inflated by the wind to give it shape.

Cells are sections of the kite body found only on box and soft kites; this Flowform has four cells, running across the kite

Fins, or keels, are triangular and make the kite more stable

A bridle consisting of lines, or legs, attached to the kite face holds the kite at the correct angle to the wind

A stabilizing cup- or cone-shaped drogue is attached to the bottom of the kite to hold it into the wind

Wide angular nose

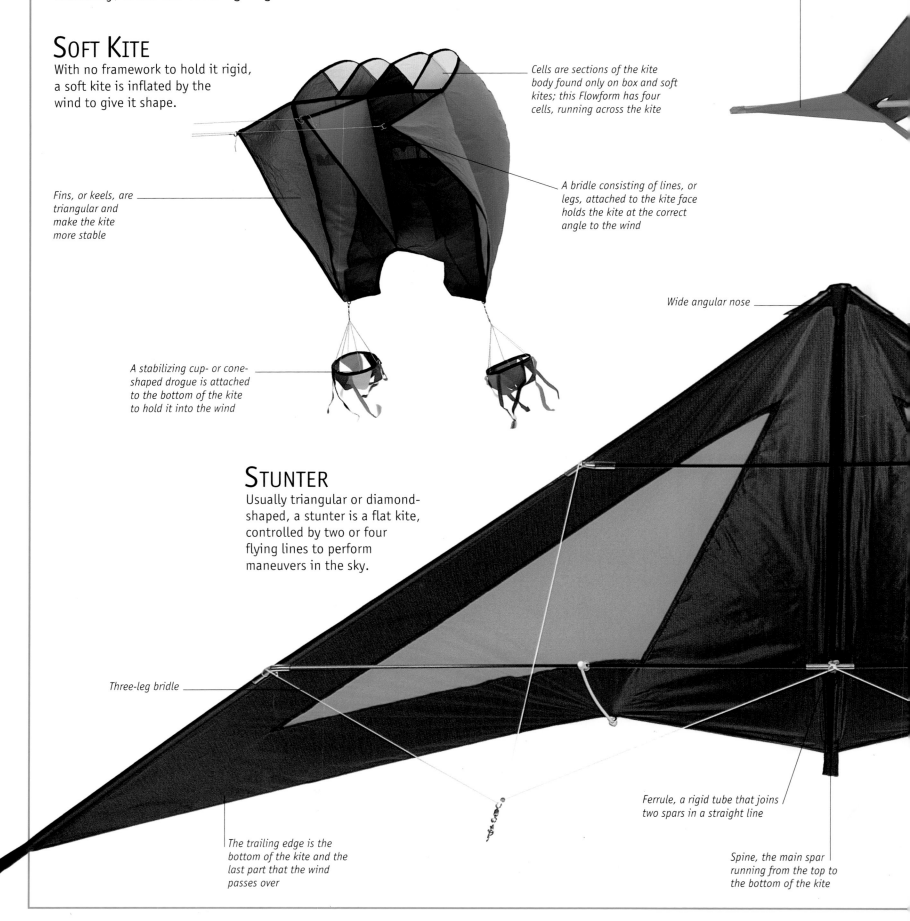

STUNTER

Usually triangular or diamond-shaped, a stunter is a flat kite, controlled by two or four flying lines to perform maneuvers in the sky.

Three-leg bridle

The trailing edge is the bottom of the kite and the last part that the wind passes over

Ferrule, a rigid tube that joins two spars in a straight line

Spine, the main spar running from the top to the bottom of the kite

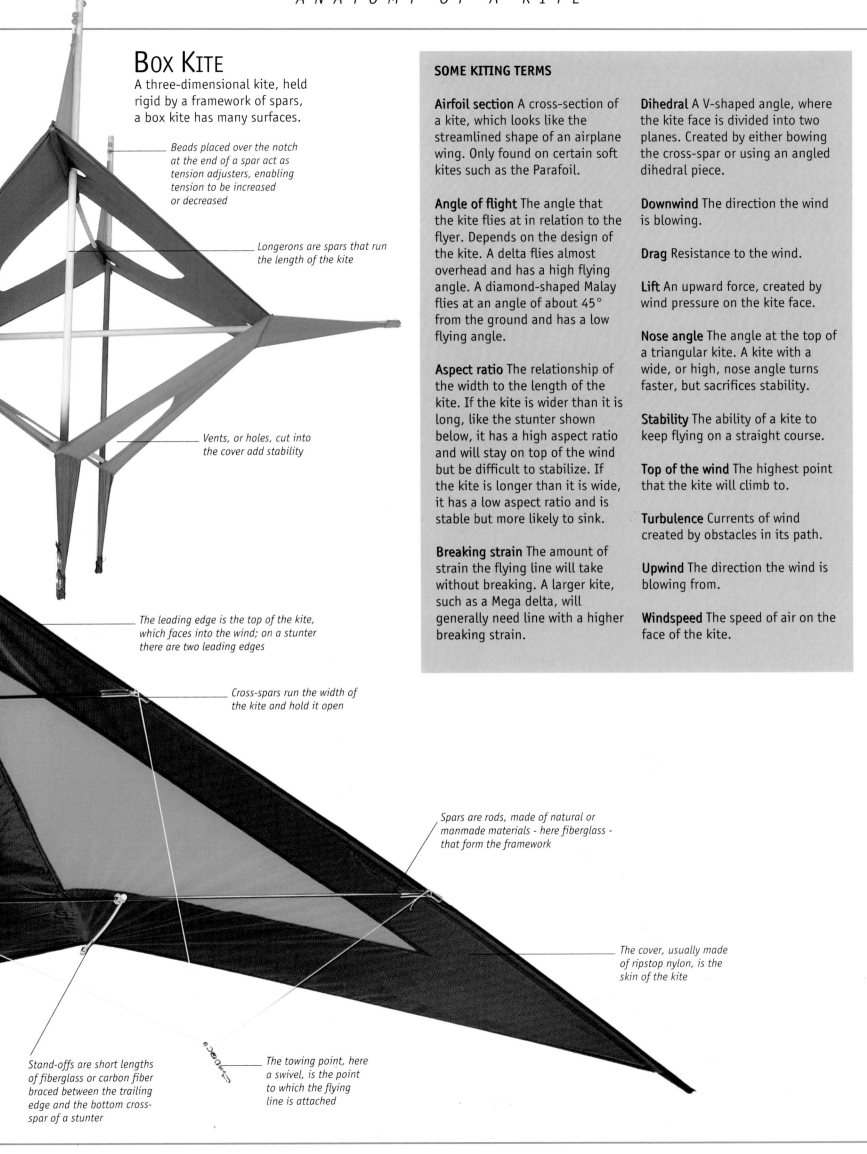

BOX KITE
A three-dimensional kite, held rigid by a framework of spars, a box kite has many surfaces.

Beads placed over the notch at the end of a spar act as tension adjusters, enabling tension to be increased or decreased

Longerons are spars that run the length of the kite

Vents, or holes, cut into the cover add stability

The leading edge is the top of the kite, which faces into the wind; on a stunter there are two leading edges

Cross-spars run the width of the kite and hold it open

Spars are rods, made of natural or manmade materials - here fiberglass - that form the framework

The cover, usually made of ripstop nylon, is the skin of the kite

Stand-offs are short lengths of fiberglass or carbon fiber braced between the trailing edge and the bottom cross-spar of a stunter

The towing point, here a swivel, is the point to which the flying line is attached

SOME KITING TERMS

Airfoil section A cross-section of a kite, which looks like the streamlined shape of an airplane wing. Only found on certain soft kites such as the Parafoil.

Angle of flight The angle that the kite flies at in relation to the flyer. Depends on the design of the kite. A delta flies almost overhead and has a high flying angle. A diamond-shaped Malay flies at an angle of about 45° from the ground and has a low flying angle.

Aspect ratio The relationship of the width to the length of the kite. If the kite is wider than it is long, like the stunter shown below, it has a high aspect ratio and will stay on top of the wind but be difficult to stabilize. If the kite is longer than it is wide, it has a low aspect ratio and is stable but more likely to sink.

Breaking strain The amount of strain the flying line will take without breaking. A larger kite, such as a Mega delta, will generally need line with a higher breaking strain.

Dihedral A V-shaped angle, where the kite face is divided into two planes. Created by either bowing the cross-spar or using an angled dihedral piece.

Downwind The direction the wind is blowing.

Drag Resistance to the wind.

Lift An upward force, created by wind pressure on the kite face.

Nose angle The angle at the top of a triangular kite. A kite with a wide, or high, nose angle turns faster, but sacrifices stability.

Stability The ability of a kite to keep flying on a straight course.

Top of the wind The highest point that the kite will climb to.

Turbulence Currents of wind created by obstacles in its path.

Upwind The direction the wind is blowing from.

Windspeed The speed of air on the face of the kite.

TRADITIONAL KITES

O ften highly decorative and emblazoned with drag-
ons, serpents and other legendary creatures or
characters, traditional kites are flown in festivals all
over the world. Many come from the Far East, where
kite-flying can be traced back for thousands of years.
Some, such as the Chinese centipede, are almost exact
copies of the original design; others are a variation,
where perhaps modern materials have been used in the
construction, or the face of the kite made more decorative. Traditional kites are exported to the West,
although the cheaper mass-produced versions are
mainly used for ornament, being fragile and not
as accurately made as those manufactured in small
numbers or as special one-off designs.

Japanese Edo
An accurate miniature
version of a classic Japanese design, with a paper
cover printed in traditional style
and a split bamboo frame. The
kite is flown bowed, but because of its size it is stable in
only the lightest of winds.

Size
2½ x 3½ in (6 x 8.5 cm)
Wind strength
Very light
Level of skill
Intermediate to
advanced
Line
2-4½ lb (1-2 kg)

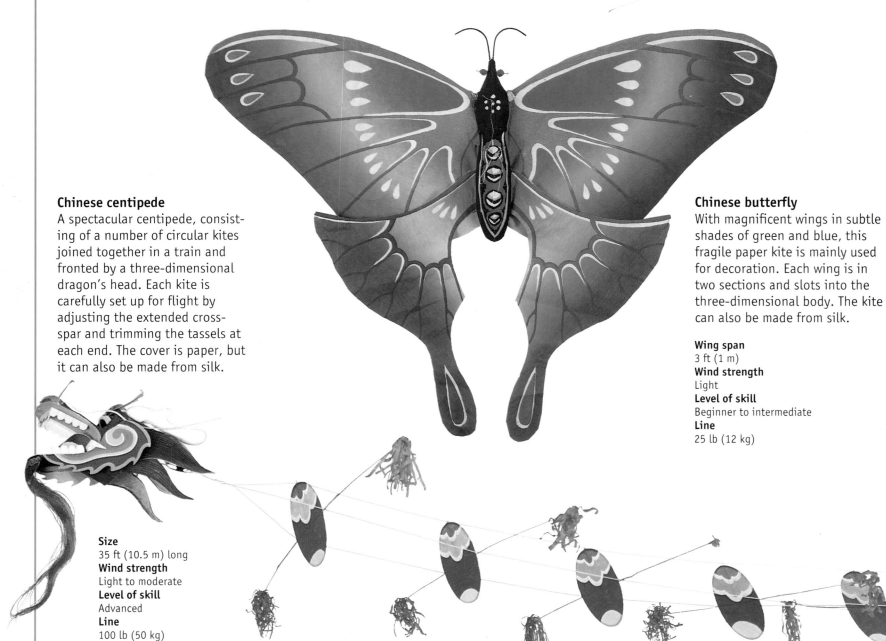

Chinese centipede
A spectacular centipede, consisting of a number of circular kites
joined together in a train and
fronted by a three-dimensional
dragon's head. Each kite is
carefully set up for flight by
adjusting the extended cross-
spar and trimming the tassels at
each end. The cover is paper, but
it can also be made from silk.

Size
35 ft (10.5 m) long
Wind strength
Light to moderate
Level of skill
Advanced
Line
100 lb (50 kg)

Chinese butterfly
With magnificent wings in subtle
shades of green and blue, this
fragile paper kite is mainly used
for decoration. Each wing is in
two sections and slots into the
three-dimensional body. The kite
can also be made from silk.

Wing span
3 ft (1 m)
Wind strength
Light
Level of skill
Beginner to intermediate
Line
25 lb (12 kg)

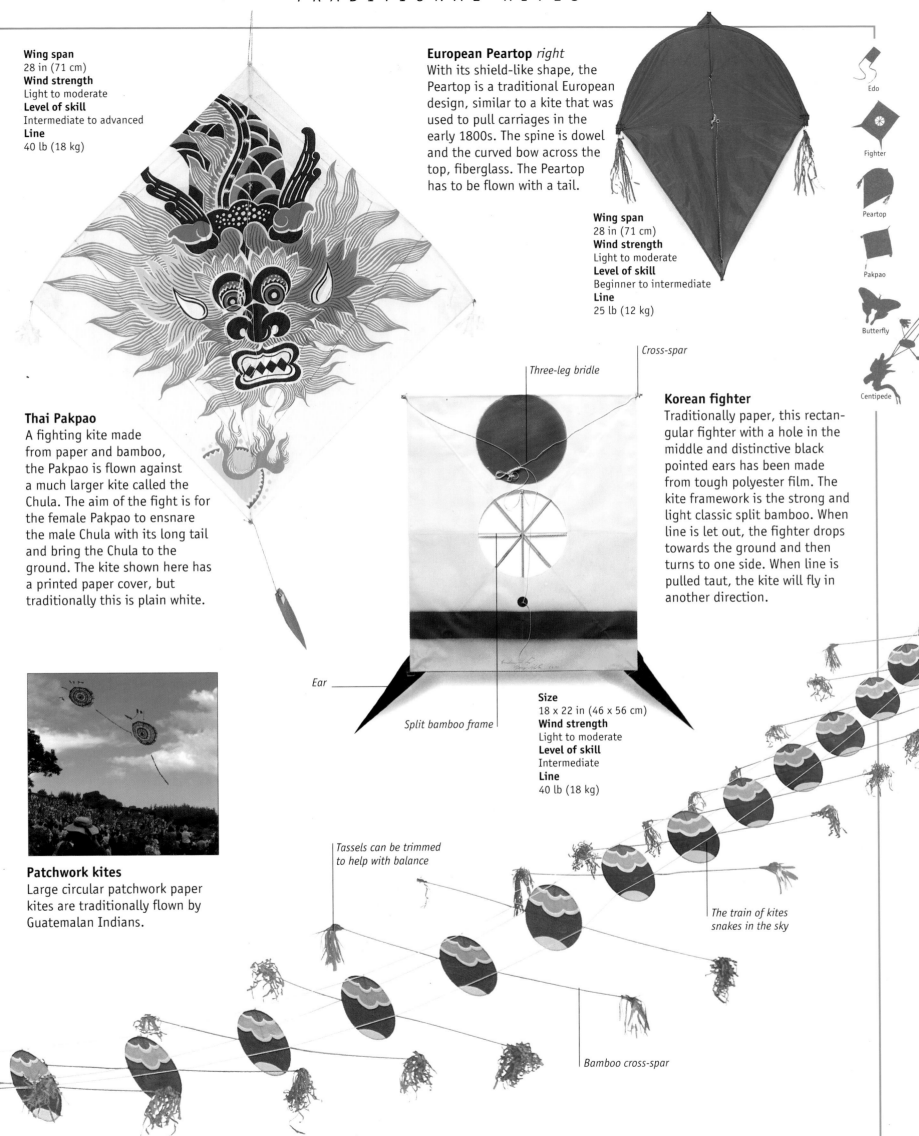

Wing span
28 in (71 cm)
Wind strength
Light to moderate
Level of skill
Intermediate to advanced
Line
40 lb (18 kg)

European Peartop *right*
With its shield-like shape, the Peartop is a traditional European design, similar to a kite that was used to pull carriages in the early 1800s. The spine is dowel and the curved bow across the top, fiberglass. The Peartop has to be flown with a tail.

Wing span
28 in (71 cm)
Wind strength
Light to moderate
Level of skill
Beginner to intermediate
Line
25 lb (12 kg)

Edo

Fighter

Peartop

Pakpao

Butterfly

Centipede

Thai Pakpao
A fighting kite made from paper and bamboo, the Pakpao is flown against a much larger kite called the Chula. The aim of the fight is for the female Pakpao to ensnare the male Chula with its long tail and bring the Chula to the ground. The kite shown here has a printed paper cover, but traditionally this is plain white.

Three-leg bridle

Cross-spar

Korean fighter
Traditionally paper, this rectangular fighter with a hole in the middle and distinctive black pointed ears has been made from tough polyester film. The kite framework is the strong and light classic split bamboo. When line is let out, the fighter drops towards the ground and then turns to one side. When line is pulled taut, the kite will fly in another direction.

Ear

Split bamboo frame

Size
18 x 22 in (46 x 56 cm)
Wind strength
Light to moderate
Level of skill
Intermediate
Line
40 lb (18 kg)

Patchwork kites
Large circular patchwork paper kites are traditionally flown by Guatemalan Indians.

Tassels can be trimmed to help with balance

The train of kites snakes in the sky

Bamboo cross-spar

FLAT KITES

T he oldest of all kites, flat kites are often very simply constructed, which leaves the face open to complex decoration. When this is coupled with a long colorful tail, the kite looks spectacular in the sky. Flat kites are inherently unstable. Without some form of added stability, they will spin and fall from the sky. One way to achieve this stability is to add a tail, which keeps the kite pointing into the wind by adding drag, or resistance, to the rear. With a tail, too, these kites will often fly in much stronger winds than many other kites. Another way of gaining stability is to use light cross-spars, which allow the wind to bow them back, creating a curved shape.

Size
4 ft (1.2 m) across
Wind strength
Moderate
Level of skill
Intermediate
Line
60 lb (27 kg)

Sode
This attractively appliquéd kite is inspired by the Japanese kimono. It has no tail but instead gains stability by three light cross-spars, which hold the face open at the top, bottom and across the middle, and give it a natural curve in flight. The spine runs down the center.

Della Porta
A very simple rectangular kite, with two diagonal spars and a long loop tail for stability. Each end of the tail is attached to a side at the bottom of the kite. If the kite begins to turn to one side, the tail becomes effectively longer on the other side and so pulls the kite back into the wind.

Size
17³/₄ x 27½ in (45 x 70 cm)
Wind strength
Light to strong
Level of skill
Beginner
Line
25 lb (12 kg)

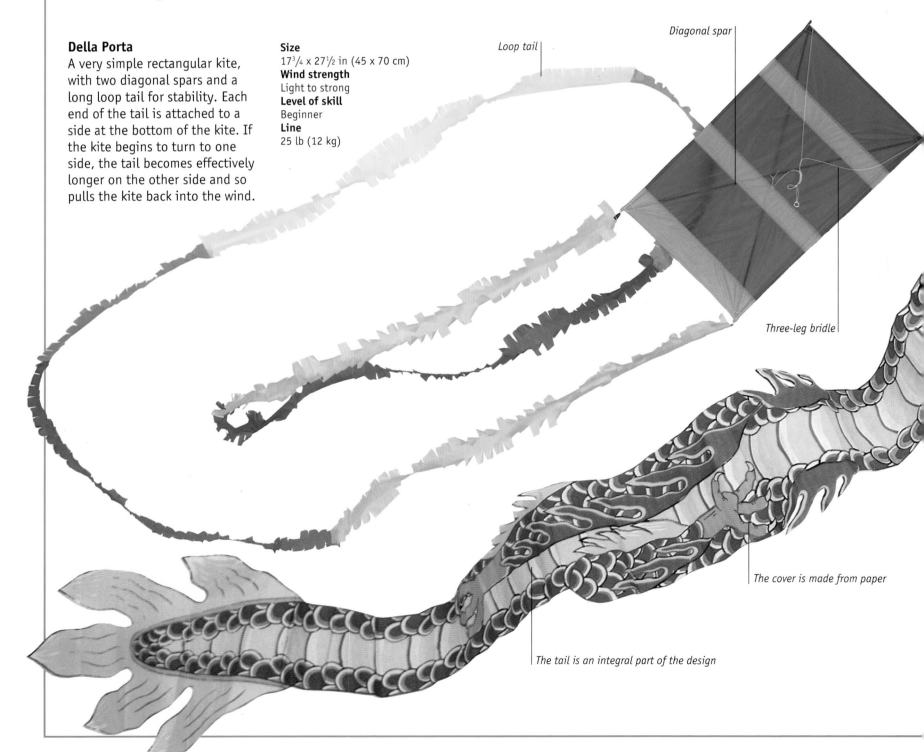

Loop tail

Diagonal spar

Three-leg bridle

The cover is made from paper

The tail is an integral part of the design

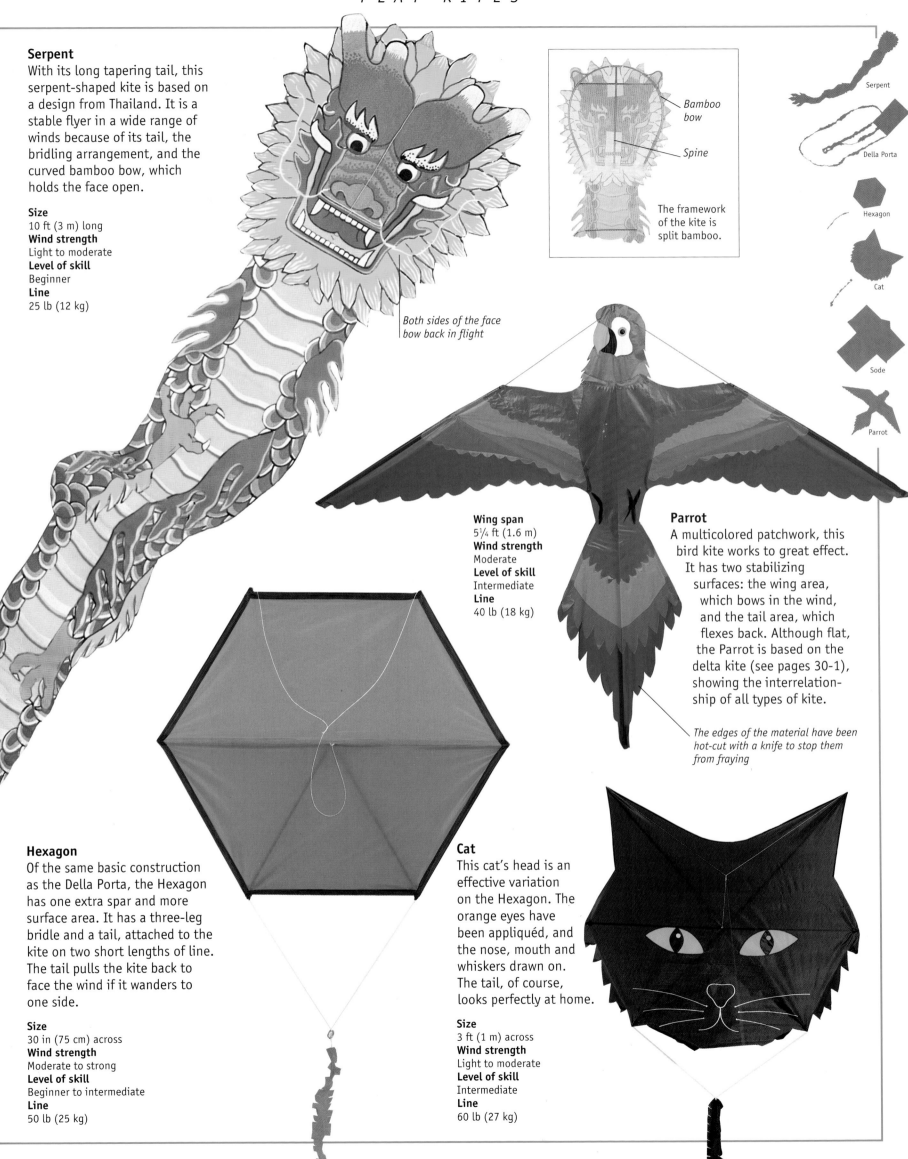

Serpent

With its long tapering tail, this serpent-shaped kite is based on a design from Thailand. It is a stable flyer in a wide range of winds because of its tail, the bridling arrangement, and the curved bamboo bow, which holds the face open.

Size
10 ft (3 m) long
Wind strength
Light to moderate
Level of skill
Beginner
Line
25 lb (12 kg)

Both sides of the face bow back in flight

Bamboo bow

Spine

The framework of the kite is split bamboo.

Serpent

Della Porta

Hexagon

Cat

Sode

Parrot

Wing span
5¼ ft (1.6 m)
Wind strength
Moderate
Level of skill
Intermediate
Line
40 lb (18 kg)

Parrot

A multicolored patchwork, this bird kite works to great effect. It has two stabilizing surfaces: the wing area, which bows in the wind, and the tail area, which flexes back. Although flat, the Parrot is based on the delta kite (see pages 30-1), showing the interrelationship of all types of kite.

The edges of the material have been hot-cut with a knife to stop them from fraying

Hexagon

Of the same basic construction as the Della Porta, the Hexagon has one extra spar and more surface area. It has a three-leg bridle and a tail, attached to the kite on two short lengths of line. The tail pulls the kite back to face the wind if it wanders to one side.

Size
30 in (75 cm) across
Wind strength
Moderate to strong
Level of skill
Beginner to intermediate
Line
50 lb (25 kg)

Cat

This cat's head is an effective variation on the Hexagon. The orange eyes have been appliquéd, and the nose, mouth and whiskers drawn on. The tail, of course, looks perfectly at home.

Size
3 ft (1 m) across
Wind strength
Light to moderate
Level of skill
Intermediate
Line
60 lb (27 kg)

BOWED & DIHEDRAL KITES

These kites have built-in stability because of the curved shape of the kite face and so are less reliant on tails than flat kites. This shape is created by either bowing the cross-spar or using an angled dihedral piece, into which the cross-spar slots. The surface of the kite is thus split into two planes. If the kite turns to one side, then that plane offers more surface area to the wind so the kite is blown back into position.

Complex six-legged bridle, allowing adjustment of the flight angle

Diamond

Otherwise known as the Malay, or Eddy bow kite, the Diamond is the classic kite-shaped kite, and is one of the most popular kites today. To give it stability, it is mostly flown bowed or with a dihedral piece, but it can be flown flat with a long tail.

Wing span
31½ in (80 cm)
Wind strength
Light to moderate
Level of skill
Beginner
Line
25 lb (12 kg)

Yakko

A traditional Japanese design in modern materials, the Yakko has an appliquéd ripstop nylon face, framed by a fiberglass hoop. In flight, the wind flexes this back at the bottom and also blows through the vents on either side, making a curved shape.

Size
33 in (84 cm) across
Wind strength
Light to moderate
Level of skill
Beginner
Line
25 lb (12 kg)

Vent

Rokkaku *above*

A traditional Japanese design, the Rokkaku is very stable because of its two bowed cross-spars, and needs little attention in the sky. It has become increasingly popular as a fighter in competitions worldwide.

Size
5¼ x 6½ ft (1.6 x 2 m)
Wind strength
Moderate
Level of skill
Beginner to intermediate
Line
200 lb (90 kg)

20

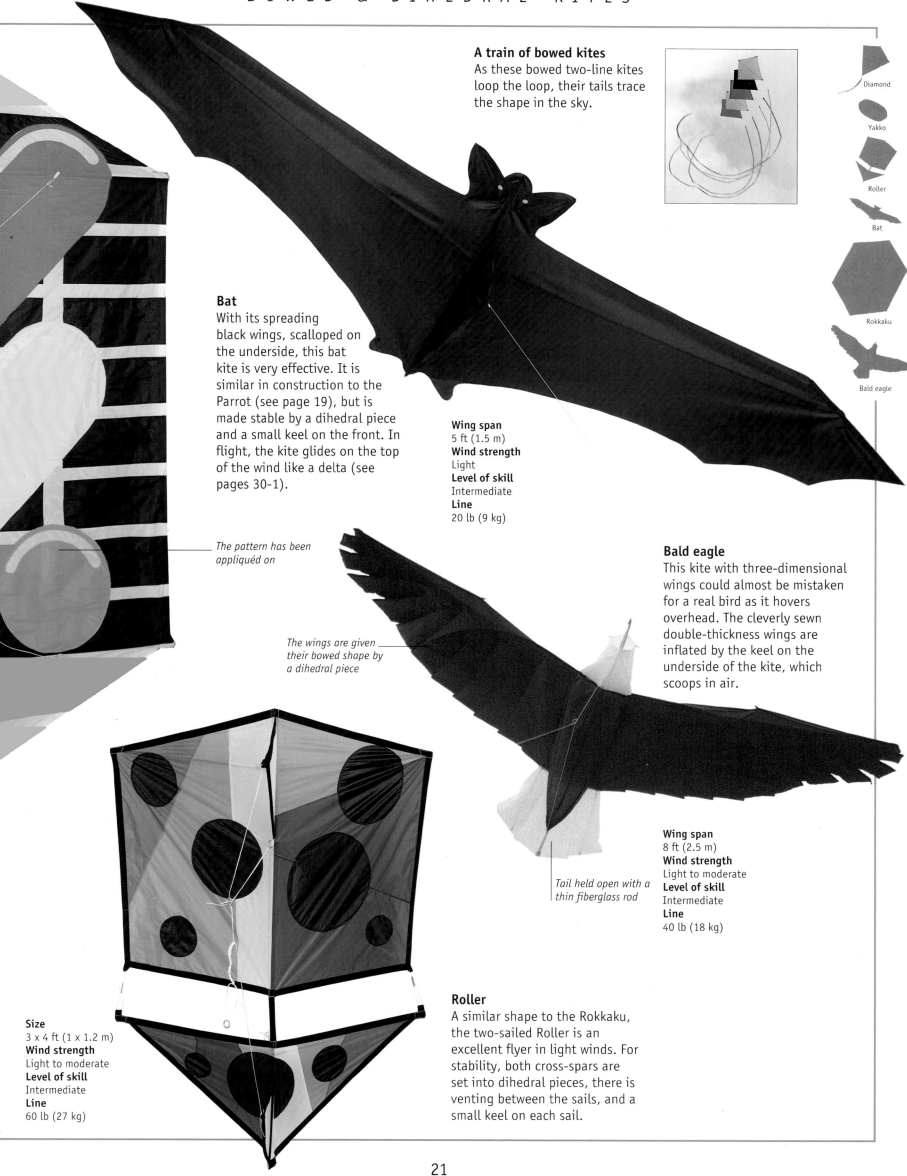

A train of bowed kites
As these bowed two-line kites loop the loop, their tails trace the shape in the sky.

Diamond

Yakko

Roller

Bat

Rokkaku

Bald eagle

Bat
With its spreading black wings, scalloped on the underside, this bat kite is very effective. It is similar in construction to the Parrot (see page 19), but is made stable by a dihedral piece and a small keel on the front. In flight, the kite glides on the top of the wind like a delta (see pages 30-1).

Wing span
5 ft (1.5 m)
Wind strength
Light
Level of skill
Intermediate
Line
20 lb (9 kg)

The pattern has been appliquéd on

The wings are given their bowed shape by a dihedral piece

Bald eagle
This kite with three-dimensional wings could almost be mistaken for a real bird as it hovers overhead. The cleverly sewn double-thickness wings are inflated by the keel on the underside of the kite, which scoops in air.

Wing span
8 ft (2.5 m)
Wind strength
Light to moderate
Level of skill
Intermediate
Line
40 lb (18 kg)

Tail held open with a thin fiberglass rod

Size
3 x 4 ft (1 x 1.2 m)
Wind strength
Light to moderate
Level of skill
Intermediate
Line
60 lb (27 kg)

Roller
A similar shape to the Rokkaku, the two-sailed Roller is an excellent flyer in light winds. For stability, both cross-spars are set into dihedral pieces, there is venting between the sails, and a small keel on each sail.

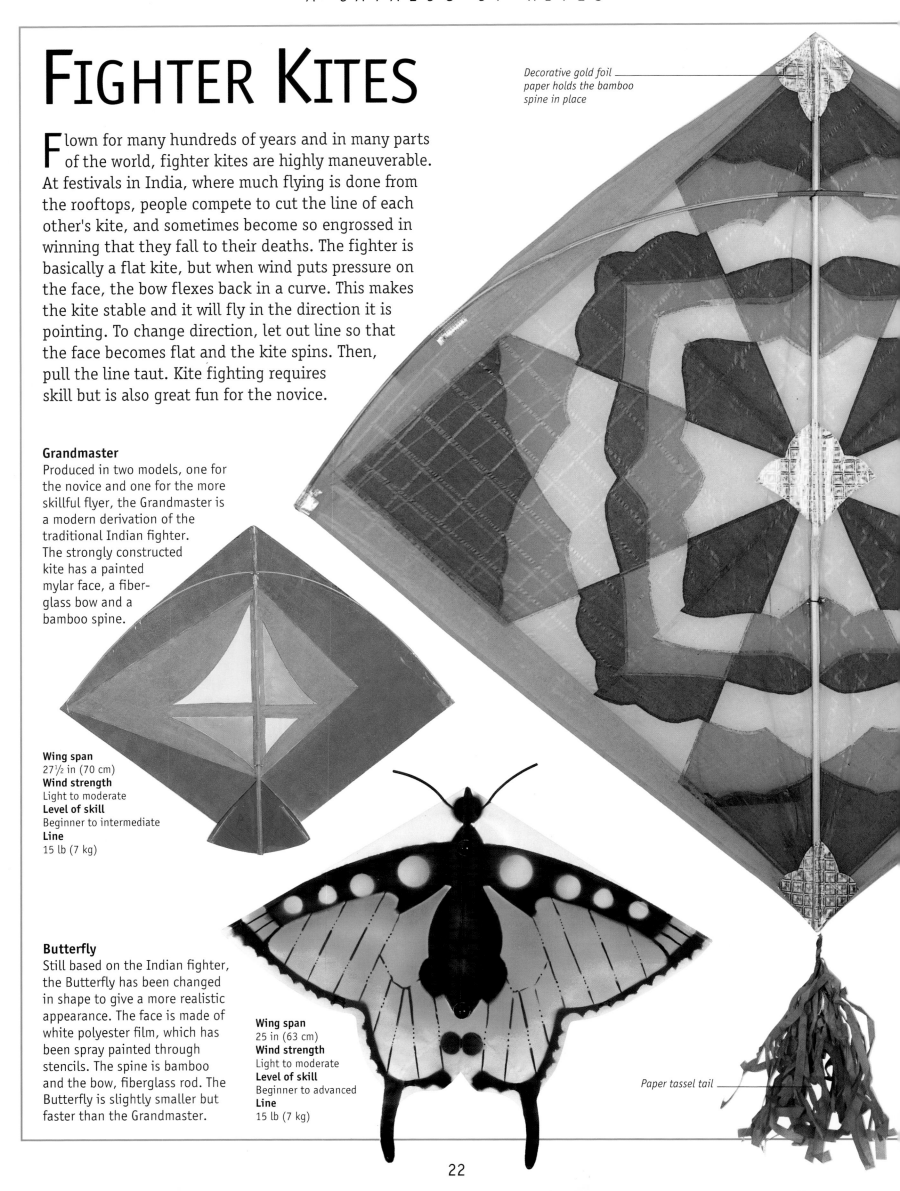

FIGHTER KITES

Flown for many hundreds of years and in many parts of the world, fighter kites are highly maneuverable. At festivals in India, where much flying is done from the rooftops, people compete to cut the line of each other's kite, and sometimes become so engrossed in winning that they fall to their deaths. The fighter is basically a flat kite, but when wind puts pressure on the face, the bow flexes back in a curve. This makes the kite stable and it will fly in the direction it is pointing. To change direction, let out line so that the face becomes flat and the kite spins. Then, pull the line taut. Kite fighting requires skill but is also great fun for the novice.

Decorative gold foil paper holds the bamboo spine in place

Grandmaster
Produced in two models, one for the novice and one for the more skillful flyer, the Grandmaster is a modern derivation of the traditional Indian fighter. The strongly constructed kite has a painted mylar face, a fiberglass bow and a bamboo spine.

Wing span
27½ in (70 cm)
Wind strength
Light to moderate
Level of skill
Beginner to intermediate
Line
15 lb (7 kg)

Butterfly
Still based on the Indian fighter, the Butterfly has been changed in shape to give a more realistic appearance. The face is made of white polyester film, which has been spray painted through stencils. The spine is bamboo and the bow, fiberglass rod. The Butterfly is slightly smaller but faster than the Grandmaster.

Wing span
25 in (63 cm)
Wind strength
Light to moderate
Level of skill
Beginner to advanced
Line
15 lb (7 kg)

Paper tassel tail

22

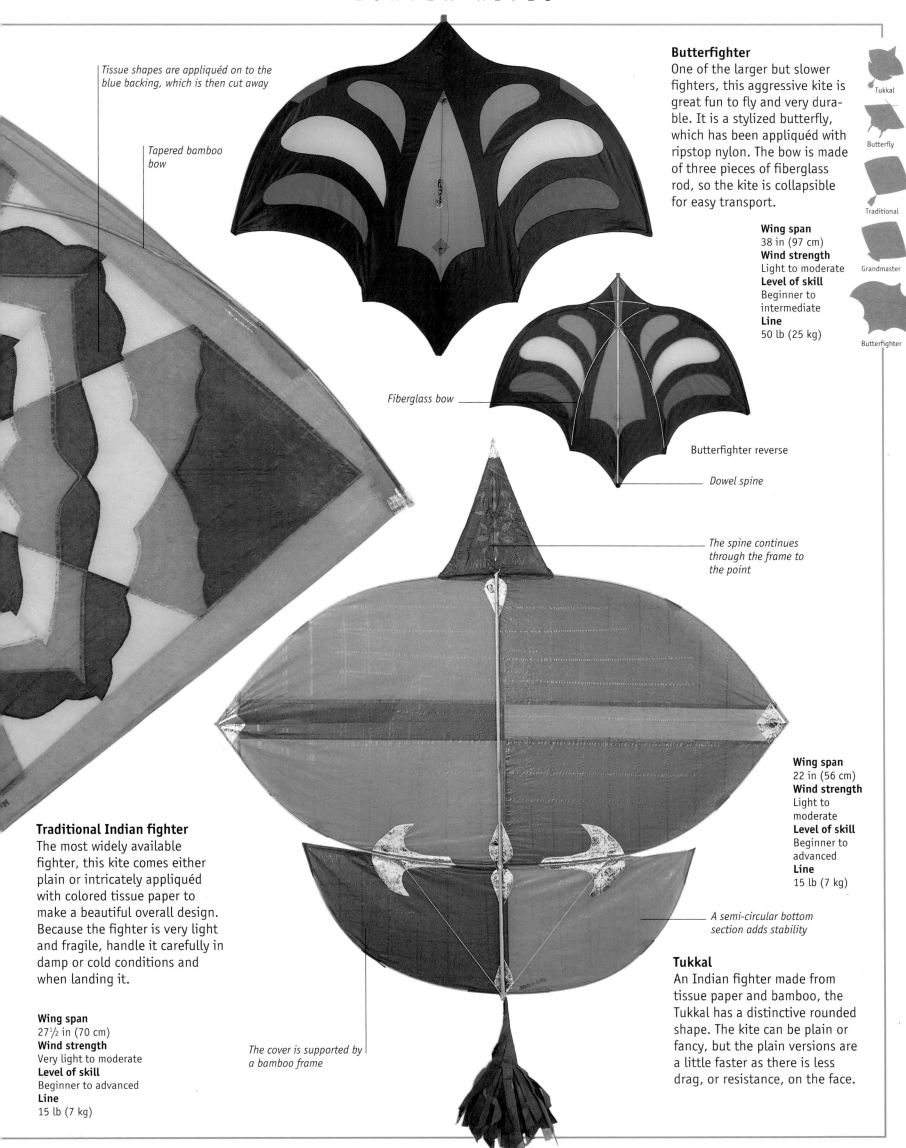

Tissue shapes are appliquéd on to the blue backing, which is then cut away

Tapered bamboo bow

Butterfighter
One of the larger but slower fighters, this aggressive kite is great fun to fly and very durable. It is a stylized butterfly, which has been appliquéd with ripstop nylon. The bow is made of three pieces of fiberglass rod, so the kite is collapsible for easy transport.

Wing span
38 in (97 cm)
Wind strength
Light to moderate
Level of skill
Beginner to intermediate
Line
50 lb (25 kg)

Tukkal

Butterfly

Traditional

Grandmaster

Butterfighter

Fiberglass bow

Butterfighter reverse

Dowel spine

The spine continues through the frame to the point

Traditional Indian fighter
The most widely available fighter, this kite comes either plain or intricately appliquéd with colored tissue paper to make a beautiful overall design. Because the fighter is very light and fragile, handle it carefully in damp or cold conditions and when landing it.

Wing span
27½ in (70 cm)
Wind strength
Very light to moderate
Level of skill
Beginner to advanced
Line
15 lb (7 kg)

The cover is supported by a bamboo frame

Wing span
22 in (56 cm)
Wind strength
Light to moderate
Level of skill
Beginner to advanced
Line
15 lb (7 kg)

A semi-circular bottom section adds stability

Tukkal
An Indian fighter made from tissue paper and bamboo, the Tukkal has a distinctive rounded shape. The kite can be plain or fancy, but the plain versions are a little faster as there is less drag, or resistance, on the face.

BOX KITES

The multi-surfaced box kite is very stable and will fly in stronger winds than other kites. Invented at the end of the last century, it marked a major advance in kite design. Box kites have been used in biplane development, for weather forecasting, to protect shipping in the Second World War, and even to carry people. In recent years, the design of box kites has become very complex, but even these sophisticated aerial sculptures can still be traced back to the classic two-celled box.

Geometric box
A Tri-D in full flight with trailing windsocks.

Classic box
The basic box kite has two square cells, one above the other, and serves as a prototype for most other boxes. It is stable in a wide range of winds. The cells are held firmly by a two-leg bridle.

Size
15 in x 3 ft (38 cm x 1 m)
Wind strength
Fairly light to strong
Level of skill
Beginner
Line
25 lb (12 kg)

Rhomboid
A variation on the standard two-celled box, the three-celled Rhomboid presents more area to the wind and so flies in even quite light windspeeds. Because of the small wings, or jibs, the spars pass outside the cover of the kite, putting an even tension across the whole cell.

Size
3½ x 4½ ft (1.1 x 1.4 m)
Wind strength
Light to strong
Level of skill
Intermediate
Line
50 lb (25 kg)

Spars run the full length of the kite

Cody
A stable flyer with the aesthetics of a vintage model, the Cody was designed and built early this century to be used as a manlifter for British army reconnaissance. It is still very popular today.

Wing span
4 ft (1.2 m)
Wind strength
Moderate
Level of skill
Intermediate
Line
60 lb (27 kg)

Wings on each cell improve flight

Brass tube

Classic box

Tri-D

Rhomboid

Cody

Harlequin

Harlequin

This giant box kite derives its name from the bold pink, green and black diamond-shaped panels, which are reminiscent of the costume of the harlequins. The thick dowel spars are joined by brass tubes, allowing the kite to be collapsed easily.

Wing span
5¹⁄₂ ft (1.7 m)
Wind strength
Fairly light to moderate
Level of skill
Intermediate
Line
100 lb (50 kg)

From the side, the cells of the Harlequin are like two Vs, running into each other.

Tri-D

Although the Tri-D looks very different, it is a variation on a two-celled box, with a pair of wings on each cell. A great modification is the single point bridle on the front cell; in gusty winds, the rear cell simply rides the gusts.

Wing span
3 ft (1 m)
Wind strength
Light to moderate
Level of skill
Intermediate
Line
50 lb (25 kg)

Tow ring for single point bridle

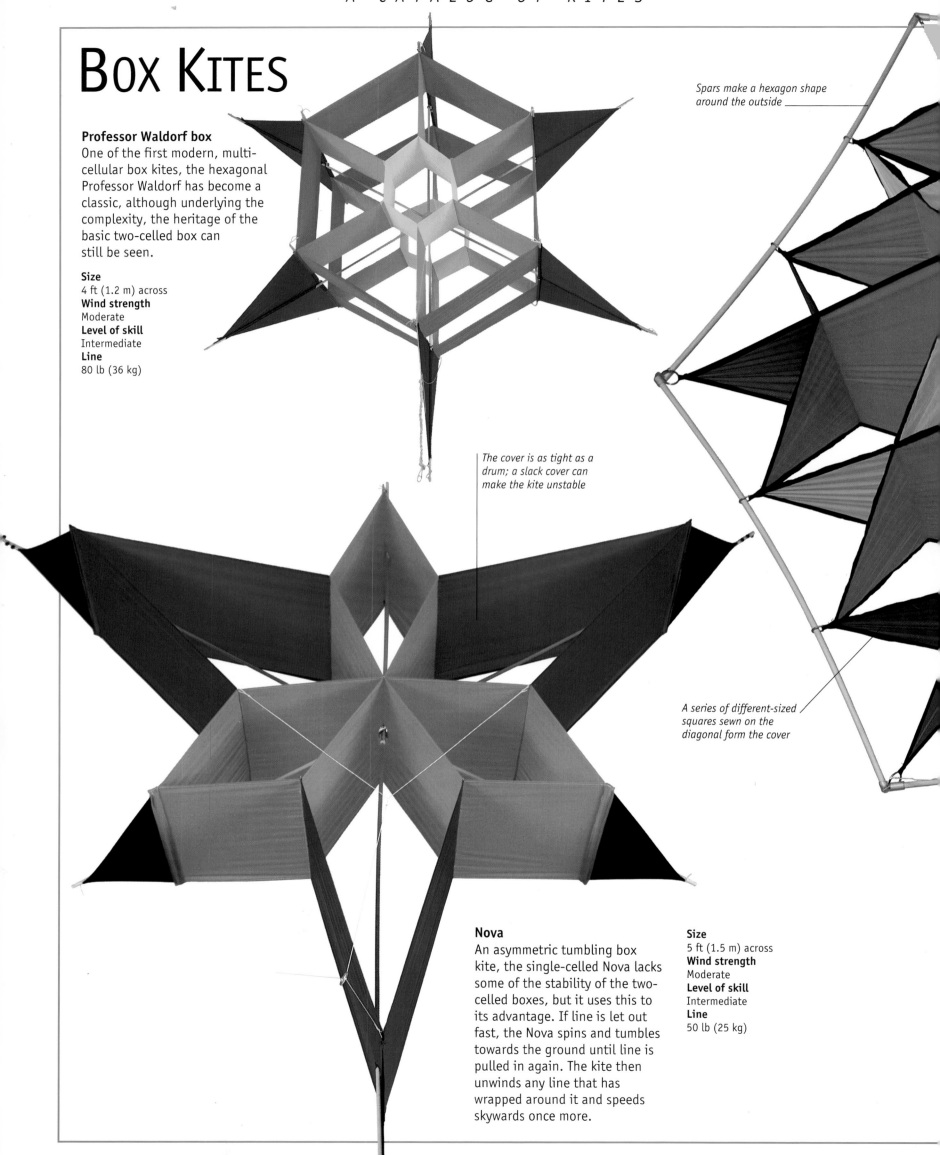

BOX KITES

Professor Waldorf box
One of the first modern, multi-cellular box kites, the hexagonal Professor Waldorf has become a classic, although underlying the complexity, the heritage of the basic two-celled box can still be seen.

Size
4 ft (1.2 m) across
Wind strength
Moderate
Level of skill
Intermediate
Line
80 lb (36 kg)

Spars make a hexagon shape around the outside

The cover is as tight as a drum; a slack cover can make the kite unstable

A series of different-sized squares sewn on the diagonal form the cover

Nova
An asymmetric tumbling box kite, the single-celled Nova lacks some of the stability of the two-celled boxes, but it uses this to its advantage. If line is let out fast, the Nova spins and tumbles towards the ground until line is pulled in again. The kite then unwinds any line that has wrapped around it and speeds skywards once more.

Size
5 ft (1.5 m) across
Wind strength
Moderate
Level of skill
Intermediate
Line
50 lb (25 kg)

Facet
This single-celled kite looks very
complicated - like an inside-out
box kite - but is actually an
extremely simple design. Unlike
the classic two-celled box, the
Facet is externally braced, the
sticks running round the outside of the kite, rather than
passing through it.

Size
5 ft (1.5 m) across
Wind strength
Moderate
Level of skill
Intermediate
Line
100 lb (50 kg)

Mini flaix

Tri-star

Prof. Waldorf

Nova

Facet

Three-leg bridle

Mini flaix *above*
A single-celled box kite with
external bracing. The spars meet
in a diamond on the outside and
the star-shaped cover is inside.

Size
26 in (65 cm) across
Wind strength
Light to moderate
Level of skill
Beginner
Line
25 lb (12 kg)

Tri-star *right*
Although the Tri-star is externally braced, it is still a variation
on the classic two-celled box,
with two triangular box
sections in the center of
the kite.

Size
3½ ft (1.1 m) across
Wind strength
Light to moderate
Level of skill
Intermediate
Line
50 lb (25 kg)

27

SLED KITES

When it was introduced, the flexible sled kite was quite a departure from the usual design of a kite because it is only supported along its length and relies on the wind to hold it open in flight. The basic sled was patented in the 1950s and there have been only fairly superficial alterations since then. Because of its simplicity, the sled is one of the most popular kites to make, and almost any light materials can be used in its construction: paper, ripstop nylon, even a plastic bag will serve as a cover, with spars made of dowel or perhaps drinking straws. The sled is fairly stable in flight but a cross-wind may push the sides of the kite together.

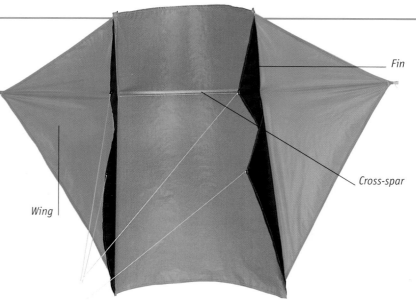

Fin

Cross-spar

Wing

Winged sled
As well as double fins, this kite has a wing on each side and a cross-spar passing through the fins. The cross-spar is not long enough to stretch the cover taut but allows it to flex in the normal way.

Wing span
4 ft (1.2 m)
Wind strength
Moderate
Level of skill
Beginner to intermediate
Line
50 lb (25 kg)

Grauel sled *left*
The basic sled had two triangular fins and no vents, but it was discovered that the kite was made more stable by cutting holes in its cover. A number of variations with vents have been tried: this one by Ed Grauel is a popular version.

Wing span
39 in (99 cm)
Wind strength
Moderate
Level of skill
Beginner to intermediate
Line
50 lb (25 kg)

Double sled
Two sleds have been joined together to form a double sled, with an extra fin in the middle. The only problem with this design is that in cross-winds, the sides vibrate in and out, making the kite look like a concertina.

Wing span
37 in (94 cm)
Wind strength
Moderate
Level of skill
Beginner to intermediate
Line
50 lb (25 kg)

Soft sled
Very light and portable, this sled is almost indestructible. Instead of spars, the kite has a tube on each side, which is inflated by the wind, to hold the cover open in the normal way.

Wing span
20 in (50 cm)
Wind strength
Moderate
Level of skill
Beginner to intermediate
Line
50 lb (25 kg)

Trailing windsock

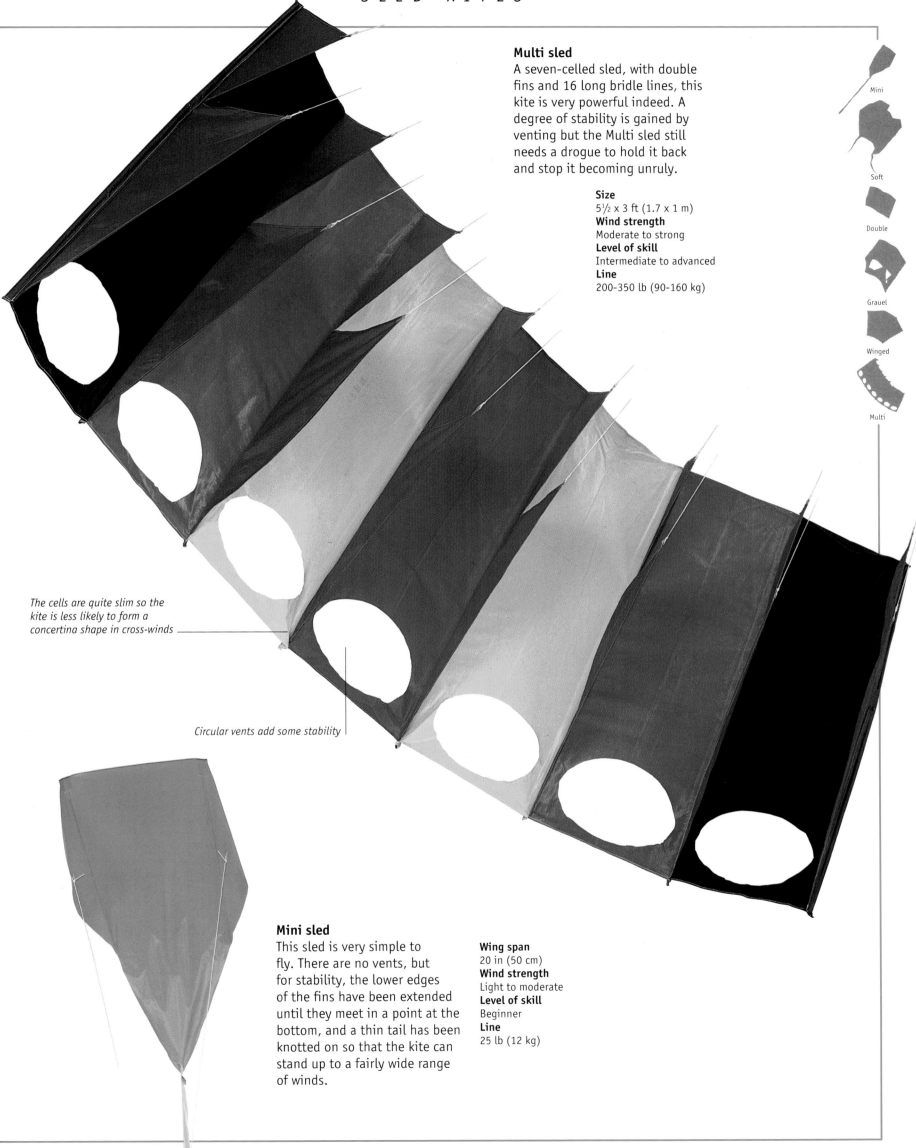

Multi sled

A seven-celled sled, with double fins and 16 long bridle lines, this kite is very powerful indeed. A degree of stability is gained by venting but the Multi sled still needs a drogue to hold it back and stop it becoming unruly.

Size
5½ x 3 ft (1.7 x 1 m)
Wind strength
Moderate to strong
Level of skill
Intermediate to advanced
Line
200-350 lb (90-160 kg)

Mini

Soft

Double

Grauel

Winged

Multi

The cells are quite slim so the kite is less likely to form a concertina shape in cross-winds

Circular vents add some stability

Mini sled

This sled is very simple to fly. There are no vents, but for stability, the lower edges of the fins have been extended until they meet in a point at the bottom, and a thin tail has been knotted on so that the kite can stand up to a fairly wide range of winds.

Wing span
20 in (50 cm)
Wind strength
Light to moderate
Level of skill
Beginner
Line
25 lb (12 kg)

DELTA KITES

With a large flexible wing area, the graceful delta is very efficient and will fly in the lightest of winds. Some deltas with very light spars will glide on thermals - rising currents of warm air - without any wind. As the thermal passes, the kite can be slowly wound in, giving enough windspeed to keep it in the air until another thermal is found. Other deltas stand up to a wide range of winds and can lift cameras.

Dan Leigh delta

A high-performance delta based on a hang-glider, the Dan Leigh flies well in even very light winds. The streamlined kite has a wide nose and an extended keel. Drag, or resistance, is not a problem as the cross-spar fits tightly, holding the cover taut.

Wing span
6½ ft (2 m)
Wind strength
Light
Level of skill
Intermediate
Line
60 lb (27 kg)

Leading edge

Fish delta

An attractively appliquéd fish kite with a keel for a fin. Where the leading edge spars finish, the cover is tapered to the nose. The tail is held open with light fiber-glass rods, like the tail of a fighter.

Wing span
5¼ ft (1.6 m)
Wind strength
Light to moderate
Level of skill
Intermediate
Line
60 lb (27 kg)

The trailing edge gently curves on either side in flight

A keel extends below the main body of the kite, adding stability

Conyne delta

A variation on a standard triangular-shaped delta, the Conyne has a box section between two spars, which gives the kite extra stability.

Wing span
9 ft (2.7 m)
Wind strength
Light to moderate
Level of skill
Beginner to intermediate
Line
50 lb (25 kg)

Leading edge

Keel

Buzzard
A life-like bird kite that is a variation on a delta, with the angled parts of the wings forming the leading edges. Most of the kite is cut away below these. The cross-spar is in two sections and joined with a dihedral piece, tied to the spine. The keel on the underside adds stability.

Fringed

Buzzard

Fish

Dan Leigh

Conyne

Mega

Wing span
5¼ ft (1.6 m)
Wind strength
Light to moderate
Level of skill
Intermediate
Line
25 lb (12 kg)

Wing span
12 ft (3.7 m)
Wind strength
Light to moderately strong
Level of skill
Intermediate
Line
200 lb (90 kg)

Mega delta
This is a standard-shaped delta with a 90° nose angle. It has a spine, two leading edge spars and a cross-spar holding the leading edge spars apart. This cross-spar does not hold the cover rigid but allows the wind to form a dihedral, or curve, along its length, giving the kite great stability.

The triangular shape is characteristic of a delta

Fringed delta
Popular with children, this delta is very easy to handle and ideal for the learner kite-flyer. A fringed trailing edge and a triangular keel add stability.

Wing span
3 ft (1 m)
Wind strength
Light
Level of skill
Beginner
Line
50 lb (25 kg)

SOFT KITES

Most soft kites are derived from the Parafoil kite, originally designed in the 1960s. This is radically different from other kites, as it has no frame to hold it rigid and is inflated by the wind. The Parafoil is basically an airfoil: a cross-section of the kite is similar to the streamlined shape of an airplane wing, improving the kite's efficiency in the air. Soft kites are very powerful and have been used to lift cameras, radios, weather-forecasting equipment and even people.

Wing span
11 ft (3.5 m)
Wind strength
Moderate
Level of skill
Intermediate to advanced
Line
200 lb (90 kg)

Snoopy stunter
Quite a complex kite composed of two Parafoils - one for each wing - and a large windsock down the center. As a stunter it is not particularly efficient but as a spectacle in the sky it is second to none.

Airfoil section

Keels sewn to the kite face held in shape by a system of bridles add stability

Tubular cell

Slow but spectacular
A kite for display, and not performance stunting, the Snoopy stunter maneuvers slowly in the sky.

Parafoil
The multi-cellular Parafoil comes in a wide range of sizes: the smallest can be held in the hand, the largest have to be held down by trucks. The number of cells and keels on each cell varies from kite to kite. The larger the kite, the greater the number of cells and keels.

Size
24 x 36 in (60 x 92 cm)
Wind strength
Moderate to strong
Level of skill
Beginner
Line
50 lb (25 kg)

Three long windsocks - wind-inflated tubes - give stability

Flowform

This has a deeper airfoil section than the Parafoil and only three keels, so the bridling is very simple. The Flowform does not pull quite as hard as the Parafoil because the rear of the kite is not held into the wind.

Size
5¾ x 6½ ft (1.75 x 2 m)
Wind strength
Light to moderate
Level of skill
Intermediate
Line
100 lb (50 kg)

The leading edge is open so the kite is inflated by the wind when airborne

V-shape cut into the trailing edge

Parafoil

Flowform

Snoopy

Octopus

Legs

Octopus

With eight tubular tails for tentacles, and large fluorescent eyes, the Octopus is a spectacular sight in the air, especially in its larger form which takes a number of people to launch. It is slightly different from the other kites shown here, as it does not have an airfoil section, but the body is inflated in a similar way.

Size
23 ft (7 m) long
Wind strength
Fairly light to moderate
Level of skill
Intermediate
Line
60 lb (27 kg)

Size
33 ft (10 m) long
Wind strength
Light to moderate
Level of skill
Intermediate to advanced
Line
1,000 lb (450 kg)

WHKF

Kicking legs

A frivolous variation on the Flowform, which has a pair of legs - the equivalent of two windsocks - attached to the rear. These are sewn to bend at the knees and kick in the air.

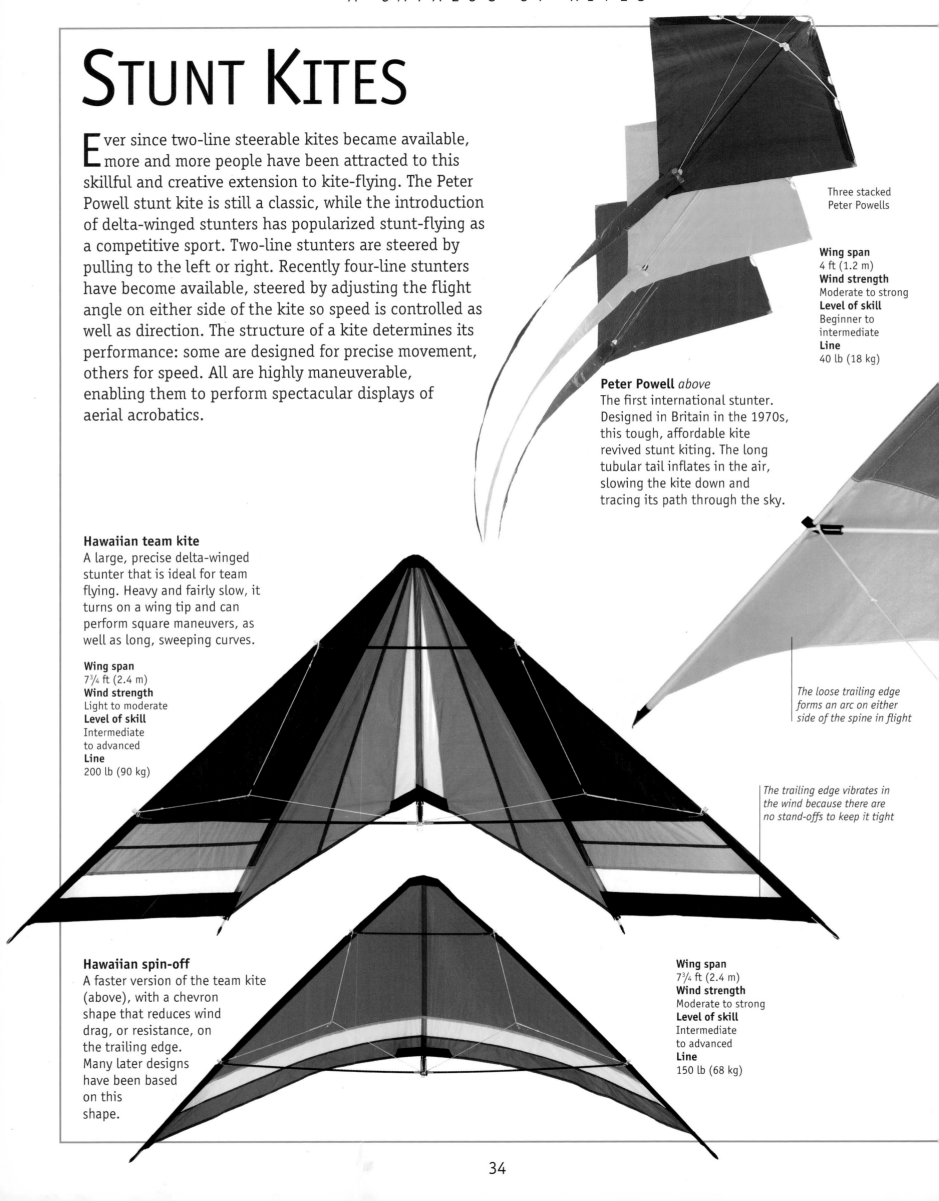

STUNT KITES

Ever since two-line steerable kites became available, more and more people have been attracted to this skillful and creative extension to kite-flying. The Peter Powell stunt kite is still a classic, while the introduction of delta-winged stunters has popularized stunt-flying as a competitive sport. Two-line stunters are steered by pulling to the left or right. Recently four-line stunters have become available, steered by adjusting the flight angle on either side of the kite so speed is controlled as well as direction. The structure of a kite determines its performance: some are designed for precise movement, others for speed. All are highly maneuverable, enabling them to perform spectacular displays of aerial acrobatics.

Three stacked
Peter Powells

Wing span
4 ft (1.2 m)
Wind strength
Moderate to strong
Level of skill
Beginner to
intermediate
Line
40 lb (18 kg)

Peter Powell *above*
The first international stunter.
Designed in Britain in the 1970s,
this tough, affordable kite
revived stunt kiting. The long
tubular tail inflates in the air,
slowing the kite down and
tracing its path through the sky.

Hawaiian team kite
A large, precise delta-winged
stunter that is ideal for team
flying. Heavy and fairly slow, it
turns on a wing tip and can
perform square maneuvers, as
well as long, sweeping curves.

Wing span
7³/₄ ft (2.4 m)
Wind strength
Light to moderate
Level of skill
Intermediate
to advanced
Line
200 lb (90 kg)

*The loose trailing edge
forms an arc on either
side of the spine in flight*

*The trailing edge vibrates in
the wind because there are
no stand-offs to keep it tight*

Hawaiian spin-off
A faster version of the team kite
(above), with a chevron
shape that reduces wind
drag, or resistance, on
the trailing edge.
Many later designs
have been based
on this
shape.

Wing span
7³/₄ ft (2.4 m)
Wind strength
Moderate to strong
Level of skill
Intermediate
to advanced
Line
150 lb (68 kg)

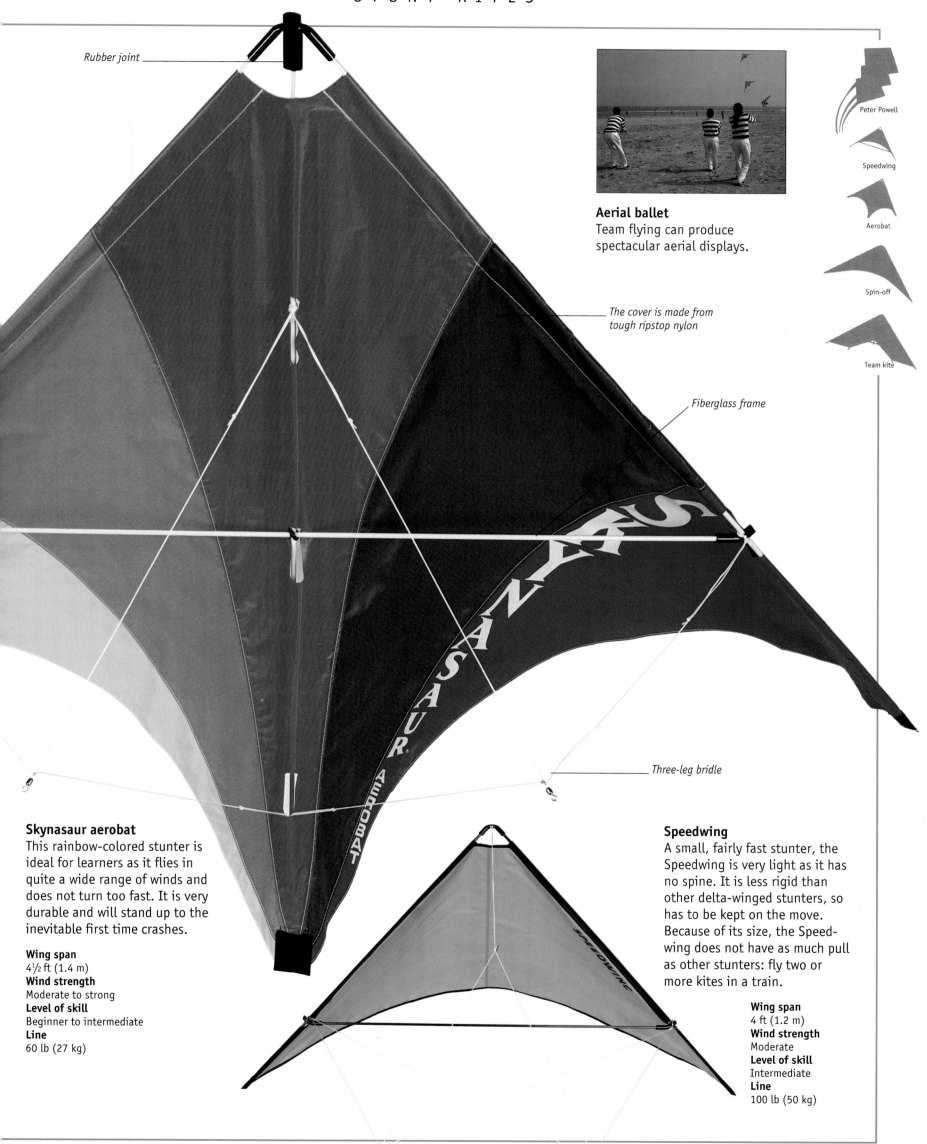

Rubber joint

The cover is made from tough ripstop nylon

Fiberglass frame

Three-leg bridle

Aerial ballet
Team flying can produce spectacular aerial displays.

Peter Powell

Speedwing

Aerobat

Spin-off

Team kite

Skynasaur aerobat
This rainbow-colored stunter is ideal for learners as it flies in quite a wide range of winds and does not turn too fast. It is very durable and will stand up to the inevitable first time crashes.

Wing span
4½ ft (1.4 m)
Wind strength
Moderate to strong
Level of skill
Beginner to intermediate
Line
60 lb (27 kg)

Speedwing
A small, fairly fast stunter, the Speedwing is very light as it has no spine. It is less rigid than other delta-winged stunters, so has to be kept on the move. Because of its size, the Speedwing does not have as much pull as other stunters: fly two or more kites in a train.

Wing span
4 ft (1.2 m)
Wind strength
Moderate
Level of skill
Intermediate
Line
100 lb (50 kg)

STUNT KITES

Carbon fiber frame

Phantom
Lightweight, fast and precise, the Phantom has a cut-away trailing edge and an extended spine, which lessen wind drag, or resistance, so the kite can turn very quickly. It is a challenge to fly and makes a spectacular sight in the air.

Carbon fiber frame

Stand-offs keep the cover tight

Wing span
6½ ft (2 m)
Wind strength
Light to moderate
Level of skill
Intermediate
to advanced
Line
150 lb (68 kg)

The top flying line attaches here

The bottom flying line attaches here

Revolution
Unlike the other stunters shown here, the Revolution is flown on four lines instead of two. Handles are attached to the lines, enabling you to adjust the bridle on each side so that the kite can fly in all directions.

Wing span
6 ft (1.9 m)
Wind strength
Moderate to strong
Level of skill
Advanced
Line
60-100 lb (27-50 kg)

Each handle is attached to a flying line at both ends. To steer the kite, move the handles up and down.

Flexifoil

A unique design, the Flexifoil is a fast, exciting kite, which is extremely powerful when flown stacked in a colorful train. The kite has a single tapered cross-spar along the leading edge. Like the Parafoil (see page 32), it relies on the wind to give it shape in flight.

Cross-spar

Cell

Paraflex

Revolution

Flexifoil

Phantom

Lite flite

Four stacked Flexifoils

Size
4-12 ft (1.2-3.7 m) across
Wind strength
Light to moderate
Level of skill
Intermediate to advanced
Line
150 lb (68 kg)

Paraflex

With many cells that are inflated by the wind in flight, the Paraflex is basically a stunting Parafoil. It is a similar shape to the Flexifoil but does not have the cross-spar. As it is totally soft, it can be taken anywhere.

Size
6 ft (1.9 m) across
Wind strength
Moderate to strong
Level of skill
Intermediate to advanced
Line
80 lb (36 kg)

The V-shape cut into the trailing edge adds stability

Lite flite

A slow, precise stunter, the Lite Flite is one of the most modern kites available. It can turn on a wing tip, and was designed for team flying in very light winds.

Wing span
7 ft (2.2 m)
Wind strength
Light to moderate
Level of skill
Intermediate to advanced
Line
80-150 lb (36-68 kg)

PAPER & PLASTIC KITES

Everyday materials such as paper and plastic lend themselves perfectly to kite-making. Newspapers, wrapping paper, even garbage bags can be used to create simple, though fragile, kites in any size. Involving little more than folding up paper or cutting a shape out of plastic, these kites are fun for children to make. Fly the kites in a light wind on sewing thread line.

Single-fold kite
The simplest paperfold kite, which is basically a rectangle of paper with a fold up the center. A single-point bridle has been threaded on and a plastic tail attached to each bottom corner of the kite. The top edge is reinforced with tape.

The center fold runs from the bottom to about two thirds of the way up

Tail made from strips of a plastic bag stuck together

Plastic sled
Two varieties of the basic sled, one made from a green garden sack with rolled up plastic spars in a contrasting color, the other cut from a shopping bag with drinking straw spars. The towing points are reinforced with tape.

Viv Comma's Kiskeedee
A kite that dances in the sky, the Kiskeedee is commercially available. Made by a Jamaican in his 70s, it has been the first kite for many thousands of children.

Plastic cover

The keel is cut at an angle

A fold runs down from each towing point to the bottom of the kite

Thin ribbon bridle

Textured artist's paper

Keeled paperfold kite
Simply a sheet of paper that has been folded in half lengthways, then each side folded up at an angle to create a keel in the middle. The back of the keel has been secured with tape and a drinking straw cross-spar added. A thin tail has been attached to the point where the keel ends.

Five-fold kite
Japanese paper speckled with silver gives an Oriental feel to the diamond-shaped face of this five-fold kite. A two-leg bridle has been added and a long tail in a contrasting color.

A smaller five-fold kite made from newspaper.

EQUIPMENT FOR FLYING

From basic handles, stunt straps and spools to some of the latest kite-flying gadgetry, such as night lights and wind-speed indicators, the choice of flying equipment is wide and at times confusing. These pages illustrate the options available, highlighting differences between similar pieces of equipment to enable you to choose the right accessories for your kite.

HANDLES

Flying line attaches here

Standard plastic handles
These lightweight handles are ideal for small kites as they may break under the strain of a larger kite being wound in.

Wooden handles
For large kites such as the Mega delta. Not for stunters.

Sky claws
A cross between a handle and a wrist strap (see above right), sky claws are good for small to medium stunters. For storage, they are slotted on to a bar, which is rotated to wind in the lines.

Heavy-duty plastic handles
More comfortable and long-lasting than the standard variety, these handles are tailor-made for medium to large stunt kites.

Flying line attaches here

The foam handle is comfortable to hold

Bar

STRAPS

Line is tied to the D-ring

Comfortable padded strap

Thin webbing strap

Wrist straps
An alternative to handles when stunting, wrist straps ease finger strain if flying for long periods. Thin straps are good for smaller stunters, padded straps for larger ones. Line cannot be stored on a strap: it has to be wound on to a spool or handle.

Wearing the strap
Slip the strap over your wrist and hold on to it below the D-ring.

Hole for index and middle fingers

Finger straps
Similar to wrist straps but worn on the fingers, these are more responsive to the feel of a stunt kite. They are only comfortable when flying in light winds.

SPOOLS & REELS

Three large holes in the center help you grip more easily

Plastic spools
Available in different sizes, circular spools allow you to let out and wind in line quickly. Not suitable for large kites as the spool will not store enough line.

Using the spool
Hold the spool vertically in one hand. To let out line, point the wider rim of the spool towards the kite. To stop line, hold the spool vertically again.

Handle, for winding in line

Wooden deep-sky reel
A heavy reel with a rotating center around which line is tied. Hold the reel in one hand, with your fingers stopping the center from moving. To release line, let go of the center.

TAILS, DROGUES & WINDSOCKS

FLYING ACCESSORIES

Gloves
Gardening gloves are ideal to stop line burning your fingers.

Night lights
To extend flying hours, battery-powered lights can be fitted on to a kite or line. They must be lightweight so that the kite's performance is not affected. Quite complex light systems are available.

Standard drogue

Drogues
Usually made of nylon, cone- or cup-shaped drogues add stability.

Sunglasses
Invest in a good quality pair; sometimes it is difficult to see the kite because of the brightness of the sky.

Line is tied to the triangle at the top

Wind-speed indicator
Basically a small propeller, held up to the wind to measure its speed at ground level.

Colorful spinning drogue, which rotates in the wind

Dog spike
This spiral of metal screws into the ground and is useful for staking a single-line kite.

Tails
Usually nylon or plastic, decorative tails stabilize the kite.

A fringed tail causes more drag, or resistance, and helps control the kite

Parachuting teddy
This brave toy is attached to the line and then parachutes to earth. A crowd-puller.

Rope handle

Pulley
Clipped over the line, this is good for retrieving large single-line kites.

Windsocks
Wind-inflated nylon or cotton tubes, trailing windsocks are attached to the bottom of the kite. They look spectacular in the sky and add stability.

Messenger
A small butterfly-shaped sail, which is attached to the bottom of the line, and flies up to the top, releasing an object such as a glider. It then slides back.

FLYING KITES

This section shows you how to launch, control and land different types of kite, with tips for overcoming common problems and faults. It explains how to assess wind conditions and choose the best place to fly. It also includes an introduction to the exciting art of stunt-flying, with instructions for classic maneuvers such as looping the loop and power diving.

HOW A KITE FLIES

A kite is heavier than air, so to fly, it needs lift, an upward force from the wind that is greater than the pull of gravity keeping it on the ground. For maximum lift, position the face at the correct angle to the wind (the angle of attack) by setting the ring accurately on the bridle. The best point for the ring is usually about a third of the way down the kite, but small adjustments can be made for varying winds. Even with the bridle pre-set, the angle of attack changes after launch, until the kite reaches its most efficient flying position.

THE ARC OF FLIGHT

In flight, the kite is affected by three main forces: lift, gravity, and drag. Lift is an upward force created by wind pressure on the face, which makes the kite rise and keeps it in the air. Gravity is the downward force on the kite, which works against lift. Drag is air resistance to the kite as it travels forwards. The sequence below shows how the angle of attack changes as the kite climbs because of the shifting relationship between forces.

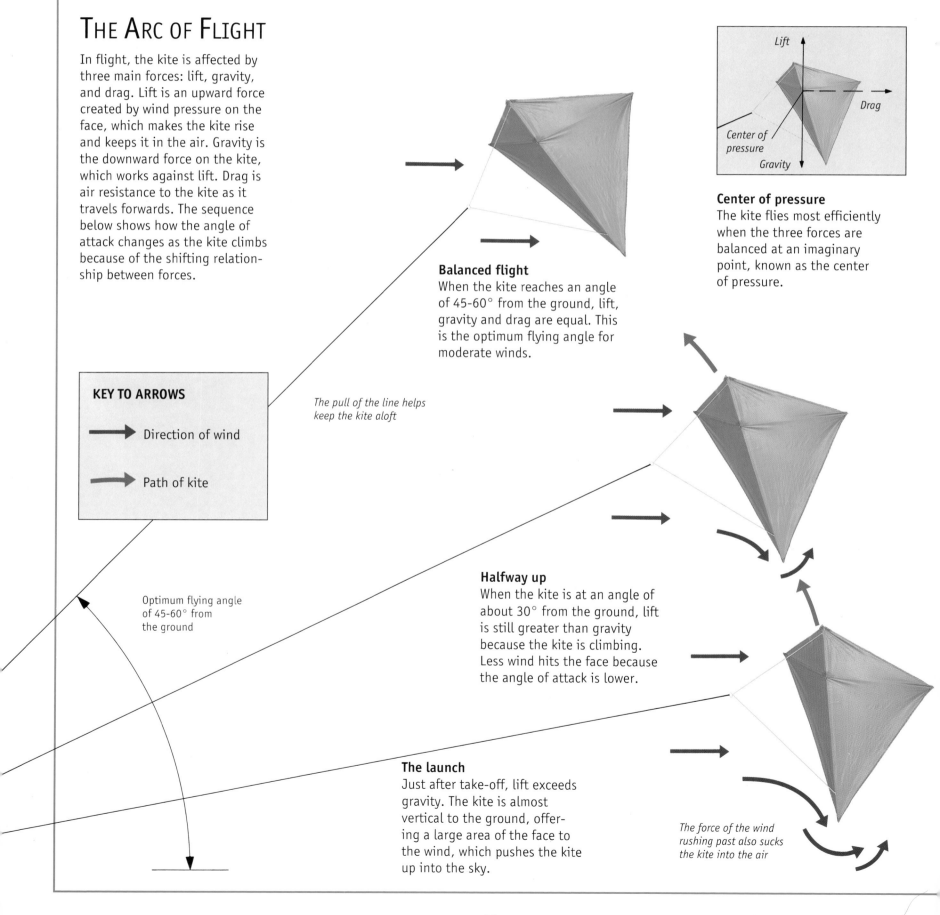

Center of pressure
The kite flies most efficiently when the three forces are balanced at an imaginary point, known as the center of pressure.

Balanced flight
When the kite reaches an angle of 45-60° from the ground, lift, gravity and drag are equal. This is the optimum flying angle for moderate winds.

The pull of the line helps keep the kite aloft

KEY TO ARROWS

→ Direction of wind

→ Path of kite

Optimum flying angle of 45-60° from the ground

Halfway up
When the kite is at an angle of about 30° from the ground, lift is still greater than gravity because the kite is climbing. Less wind hits the face because the angle of attack is lower.

The launch
Just after take-off, lift exceeds gravity. The kite is almost vertical to the ground, offering a large area of the face to the wind, which pushes the kite up into the sky.

The force of the wind rushing past also sucks the kite into the air

STAYING AIRBORNE

To remain aloft, a kite has to be kept pointing into the wind, so it requires directional stability. Some kites are inherently stable because of their design, others need stability added.

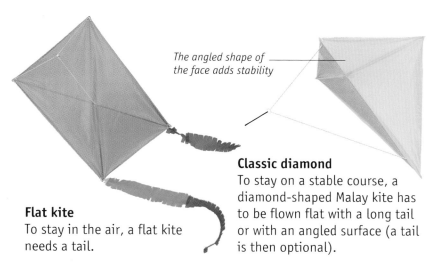

The angled shape of the face adds stability

The widest part of the kite is at the bottom

Balloon keel, which is inflated by the wind to give stability

Triangular delta
The shape of the delta and its curved trailing edge help keep the kite flying almost horizontal to the ground - a low angle of attack.

The back cell keeps the front cell facing into the wind

Flat kite
To stay in the air, a flat kite needs a tail.

Classic diamond
To stay on a stable course, a diamond-shaped Malay kite has to be flown flat with a long tail or with an angled surface (a tail is then optional).

Two-celled box
A rigid box kite has many surfaces that give the kite lift and stability.

SETTING THE BRIDLE

Position the bridle approximately first, then fine-tune it on the field.

Normal towing point

20-30°

Hold the kite by the ring

1 Lay the kite on its back. Put your finger underneath the bridle line and carefully move your hand up the line to lift the top of the kite.

2 When the top of the kite is at an angle of 20-30° from the ground, tie a ring to the place where your finger is with a lark's head knot (see page 65). The ring becomes the towing point. This is usually about a third of the way down the length of the kite and stands off from the face by about half the length.

3 Test the kite for flight by holding it into the wind. If the wind lifts the kite, the bridle is in the right position.

ADJUSTING THE TOWING POINT

The towing point may need to be adjusted to suit the wind conditions on site. However, only very slight adjustments are needed to change the angle of attack sufficiently: a maximum of ½ in (1 cm) from the normal towing point position.

Light winds
In light winds, move the ring down to expose more of the face to the wind.

Strong winds
If the wind is strong, move the ring towards the top of the kite. This will reduce wind pressure on the face.

PREPARING TO FLY

It is best to fly a kite on a flat, open site, which is free of obstructions, such as trees, buildings and overhead wires. If there are other flyers around - as there will be at festivals - choose the clearest part of the sky for launching the kite. Contrary to popular belief, you do not need a strong force of wind to make a kite fly: light to moderate breezes are best, although some kites, such as heavy boxes or more robust stunters, are designed for stronger winds. Always assess the wind speed before launching a kite.

CHOOSING A SITE

The ideal flying site is flat and without obstructions, for example a beach or a field in the countryside or a large open park in a built-up area. Any trees or buildings in the wind's path will cause turbulence.

Flying by the sea
A beach is a great location for kite-flying with often nothing but the sand and sea for miles. Avoid cliffs because of turbulence.

The freedom of flying
Kite-flying in a wide open area gives a real sense of freedom.

KITE FLYER'S SAFETY CODE
▲ Choose an open site, never within three miles of an airfield.
▲ Do not fly near telephone poles or overhead wires.
▲ Do not fly in a thunderstorm: the kite could act as a lightning conductor.
▲ Avoid people and animals.
▲ Do not fly too near other kites unless stunting or kite-fighting.
▲ Wear protective gloves, especially for larger kites and in stronger winds as line can burn hands.
▲ Do not fly your kite over the legal limit in your country.

Open space
Although not completely free of obstructions, this park is a good flying site with any buildings well away from the flyer.

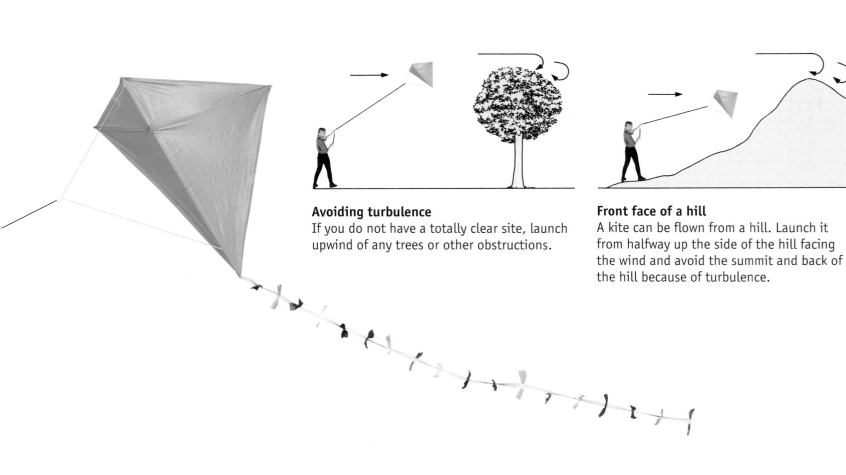

Avoiding turbulence
If you do not have a totally clear site, launch upwind of any trees or other obstructions.

Front face of a hill
A kite can be flown from a hill. Launch it from halfway up the side of the hill facing the wind and avoid the summit and back of the hill because of turbulence.

MEASURING WIND SPEED

As a general rule, most kites are designed to fly between certain windspeeds, although some will fly in a wide range of winds. To check the wind speed,either use a wind-speed indicator (see page 41) or the Beaufort Scale. This system, originally devised in 1805 by British Admiral Sir Francis Beaufort to record wind strength at sea, measures wind speed on land, using indicators such as trees and plumes of smoke. The scale starts from Force 0 (calm) and rises to Force 12 (hurricane). Do not fly a kite in winds stronger than Force 6 on the scale.

BEAUFORT WIND SCALE				
DESCRIPTION	VISUAL INDICATOR	SUITABLE KITES	WIND SPEED (m.p.h.)	FORCE
Calm	Smoke rises		under 1	0
Light air	Smoke drifts		2	1
Light breeze	Leaves rustle	A delta is good for light winds as it glides on the top of the wind.	5	2
Gentle breeze	Leaves move	Bowed kites are tailor-made for gentle to fresh winds.	10	3
Moderate breeze	Branches move		15	4
Fresh breeze	Small trees sway	Generally, box kites fly best in moderate to stronger winds.	21	5
Strong breeze	Large branches move		28	6

SINGLE-LINE KITES

Whether a box kite or a diamond-shaped Malay, single-line kites are easy to launch and retrieve. They make quite a spectacle in the sky, either let out on longer line or brought in closer to the ground. Before launching the kite, check that the bridle is set for flight (see page 45), the spars are seated securely in their pockets, the flying line is tied on properly and any tail is unravelled. Do not run with the kite to launch it, unless you want the exercise. If the kite starts to drop in the air, wind in line or step back and it will rise.

SHORT LAUNCHING

So-called because the kite is launched on a short length of line, this is the standard method for launching a single-line kite. If your kite does not lift, it is probably because it is too large, the wind is too light or there is ground turbulence, so try long launching.

LONG LAUNCHING

Launch a kite on a long length of line if short launching has failed or you are launching a large kite that is awkward to handle at close quarters. It is easiest to long launch with a helper.

Hold the kite in front of you

Hold the kite up and tilt it forwards slightly

Hold the kite at arm's length

Point the spool rim towards the kite so that line can slip off easily

Move the handle backwards and forwards to unwind line

Step back

1 Stand with your back to the wind, holding the kite in one hand and the handle or spool in the other.

2 Release the kite into the air, letting out a little line as you do so. The wind will catch the sail and lift the kite. Slowly pay out more line.

1 Hold the handle or spool, and ask your helper to take the kite and walk backwards downwind while you unravel 30-50 ft (9-15 m) of line.

2 When you give a signal, the helper should hold the kite up and gently release it. Move backwards or wind in line to help the kite climb.

STANDARD RETRIEVAL

This method can be used to retrieve a kite on a long or short flying line. With practice, the kite can be wound in so that it can be picked out of the sky, though in reality it may drop a little in front of you.

Wind in line

Spool faces kite

Let line run freely through your fingers

1 To retrieve the kite, simply wind in the flying line on to the handle or spool.

2 If turbulence causes the kite to dart around in the sky, let out line to stabilize the kite, then wind it in again.

WALKING THE KITE DOWN

If you try to bring the kite in using the standard method and find that there is too much pull, follow this procedure.

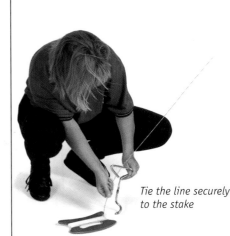

Tie the line securely to the stake

1 Anchor the flying line by tying it to a stake such as a dog spike or a tree.

3 When you reach the kite, put it on its back so that the wind will not lift it, unclip the pulley, and untie the flying line. Dismantle the kite.

2 Clip a pulley over the line, hold on to the handle below the pulley and walk downwind towards the kite. It will be pulled from the sky.

4 Go back to the anchor point and wind the flying line on to the handle or spool.

FIGHTER KITES

The competitive sport of kite-fighting goes back hundreds of years. Exciting and fun, it requires skill, quick responses and total concentration, otherwise the line of your kite will be cut by an opponent. If you are a beginner, tape a long plastic tail to the rear of your kite. This will slow down its reactions. As you become more skilled, shorten the tail. Eventually you will be able to do without one. Traditionally, fighters are flown on glass-coated line, but it is safer to use standard line for practice.

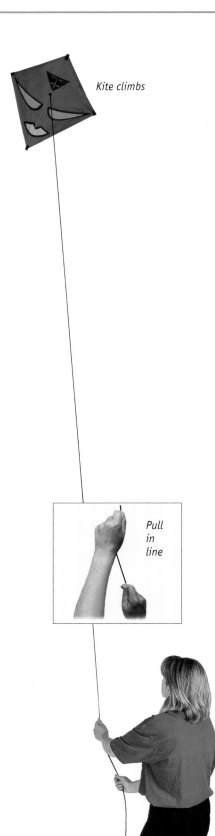

Kite climbs

LAUNCHING A FIGHTER

It is easiest to launch a fighter with the help of a friend. Always have the wind behind you.

Hold the kite in front of you

Point the spool rim towards the kite

Point the spool rim towards the ground

Pile of line

Use one hand to release the kite

Pull in line

1 Hold the handle or spool and ask your helper to take the kite and walk backwards downwind, while you unravel 30-50 ft (9-15 m) of line.

2 Let out some more line so that you have a pile at your feet. Put the handle or spool on the ground, slightly to one side of you.

3 Hold the line above the pile. When you give a signal, your helper should hold the kite up and gently let go.

4 Pull in the line hand over hand so that the kite climbs and clears ground turbulence.

MANEUVERING A FIGHTER

The closer the kite is to you, the faster your reactions will have to be, so aim to get the kite to climb to 200 ft (60 m). You will probably have to repeat the following steps several times to do this. Once the kite reaches this height, practice controlling your fighter until you can make it go where you want it to.

TIPS FOR MANEUVERING
▲ If the kite is flown far out to one side, it loses stability. Pull in line hand over hand and let it drop in the pile.
▲ Always have enough line in the pile to release suddenly if the kite dives to the ground from a low level.

RETRIEVING A FIGHTER

Simply pull in line hand over hand and let it drop in the pile at your feet.

Keep the kite out to one side when retrieving it so that it lands gently

GOING ON THE ATTACK

Lift his line by putting yours underneath

Defend yourself by releasing line from the pile

Attack your opponent by trying to cut his line

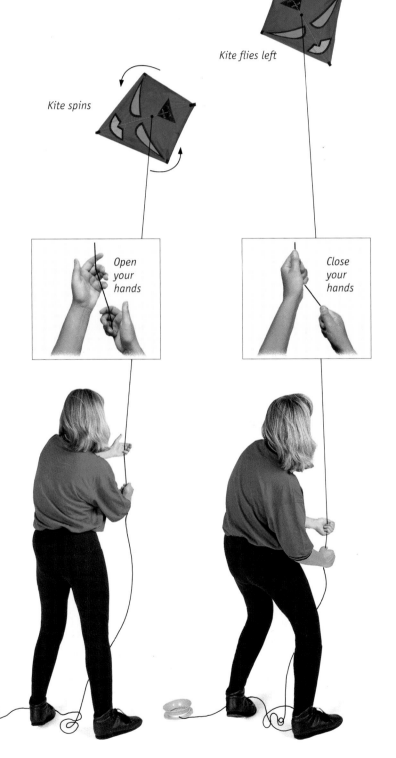

Kite flies left

Kite spins

Open your hands

Close your hands

1 Let line run freely through your fingers. The kite will spin and slowly lose height. It will travel downwind, releasing more line.

2 When the kite nose is pointing in the direction you want it to fly (up to gain height), stop the line. The kite will travel in that direction.

The aim is to cut your opponent's line before he cuts yours. To do this, move your line very quickly over his. You will be at an advantage if you can lift his line by positioning yours underneath. If he attacks you, release line from your pile so that friction from his cut is spread over more of your line.

STUNT KITES

Controlling a stunt kite in even a basic maneuver adds another dimension to kite-flying. Once a single-line kite is launched, you can enjoy the spectacle, whereas a stunter needs constant steering to stay in the sky. As a rule, the kite lines should be 150-200 ft (45-60 m) long, although you may want to shorten them as you become more experienced; the shorter the lines, the quicker your reactions will have to be. If this is your first attempt at flying a stunter, get the feel of the kite before trying any maneuvers.

SELF-LAUNCHING

Launching a stunt kite on your own is fairly simple. Always have the wind behind you, and also make sure that when the kite is laid out, the flying lines are exactly equal and not crossed.

TIPS FOR LAUNCHING
▲ During take-off, keep your hands together to steer the kite straight up.
▲ If the kite veers to either side, steer it back by pulling on the opposite line.
▲ The helper may prefer to rest the kite against his legs instead of holding it up.

Kite nose points towards you

1 Put the kite face-down on the ground, and walk backwards upwind unravelling all the line off the handles.

2 Push a stake such as a dog spike or a tent peg into the ground and place the handles over it to hold them.

3 Return to the kite. Position it on the points on its base and lean it back slightly so that it is not lifted by the wind.

Choose a different colored handle for each hand

Step back

4 Go back to the handles. Pick up the left handle in your left hand and the right handle in your right hand. Move back and the kite will take off.

LAUNCHING WITH A HELPER

Sometimes it is easiest to enlist the help of a friend when launching a stunter. Diamond-shaped stunt kites, such as the classic Peter Powell, have to be launched this way.

Hold the kite in front of you

Move the handles up and down

1 Hold the handles and ask your helper to take the kite and walk backwards downwind while you unravel all the line off the handles.

STEERING

If this is your first launch, let the kite travel as high as it will go (if you practice a maneuver too close to the ground, you may crash the kite). Then, practice these basic steering movements to get the feel of the kite. Remember that when you steer, the direction the kite flies in will depend on its position in the sky. If you pull with your right hand, the kite will not necessarily go to the right side of the sky.

Hold the kite higher

Hands level

Step back

Kite turns right

Pull right

Kite turns left

Pull left

Kite flies straight up

Hands level

2 When you give a signal, the helper should hold the kite up and gently release it. Step back to pull it away from him.

Turning right
Pull gently with your right hand. The kite will steer right relative to its starting position.

Turning left
Pull gently with your left hand. The kite will steer left relative to its starting position.

Keeping on a straight course
Hold both hands together to go straight in any direction.

SIMPLE LOOP

The most basic stunt maneuver, the loop helps you to learn control of the kite. At first keep your hands close together so that the loop is quite large. Then try a smaller loop by keeping your hands further apart. When tracing a series of loops in one direction, do the same number in the opposite direction to unwrap the lines.

Loop maneuver

INFINITY

This simple figure of eight logically follows on from the basic loop. Trace the shape in the sky again and again to perfect your technique, aiming to keep the cross-over point directly downwind of you each time.

Kite looping

Nose points up

Kite flies straight

Kite turns right

Right hand back

Hands level

Hands level

Right hand back

1 Gently move your right hand back and keep it in this position so that the kite does a loop.

2 When the nose of the kite points up, bring your hands level. Let the kite travel to the highest point it can reach.

1 Start by holding both hands level so that the kite flies in a straight line.

2 Gently move your right hand back so that the kite turns to the right.

Infinity maneuver

HELPFUL TIPS FOR INFINITY

▲ Make sure your hands are the same distance apart so that both sides of the shape are the same size.

▲ Keep all hand movements gentle for good rounded curves.

▲ Vary the size of the figure by changing your hand distance.

BASIC LANDING

The easiest way to land a stunt kite safely, this simple method is invaluable for the learner stunt-flyer.

Hands horizontal

1 Keeping one hand on top of the other, steer the kite parallel to the ground as far as it will go.

Left hand forward

Right hand close to body

Step forward

2 When the kite reaches this point, bring your left hand forward and step forward. The kite will gently drop from the sky.

Kite passes cross-over point

Kite begins to turn left

Kite begins to turn right

Hands level

Left hand back

Right hand back

3 Move your right hand forward so that it is level with the left again. The kite will pass through the cross-over point.

4 Move your left hand back so the kite turns left. Then bring your hands level; the kite will pass the cross-over point again.

5 Gently move your right hand back and complete the right hand turn, returning to step 2.

POWER DIVE

An intermediate stunt maneuver, the power dive helps you learn how to turn the kite tightly and control its speed. Start the maneuver with the kite travelling right, high off the ground and parallel to it.

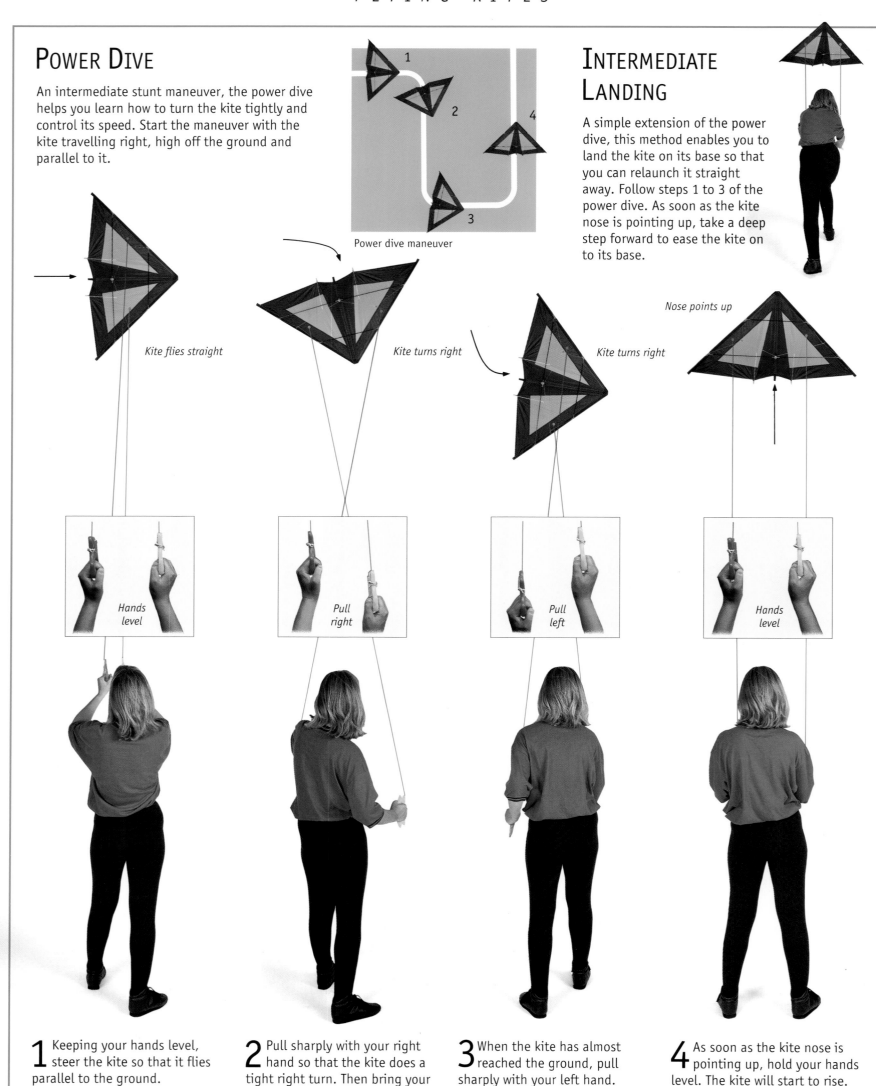

Power dive maneuver

INTERMEDIATE LANDING

A simple extension of the power dive, this method enables you to land the kite on its base so that you can relaunch it straight away. Follow steps 1 to 3 of the power dive. As soon as the kite nose is pointing up, take a deep step forward to ease the kite on to its base.

Nose points up

Kite flies straight

Kite turns right

Kite turns right

Hands level

Pull right

Pull left

Hands level

1 Keeping your hands level, steer the kite so that it flies parallel to the ground.

2 Pull sharply with your right hand so that the kite does a tight right turn. Then bring your hands level. The kite will fly towards the ground.

3 When the kite has almost reached the ground, pull sharply with your left hand. The kite will turn to your right.

4 As soon as the kite nose is pointing up, hold your hands level. The kite will start to rise. Once it reaches the top of the line, the maneuver is complete.

SQUARE

To practice the power dive in another maneuver, try the square. Start this in the same way as the power dive. Aim for crisp 90° turns and keep the sides of the square straight by holding your hands at the same distance apart. The kite speed should be consistent throughout.

Square maneuver

TIPS FOR THE MANEUVERS
▲ Initially, do not bring the kite too close to the ground as you may crash it.
▲ The kite's speed increases as it nears the ground. Move forwards to slow it down.
▲ The kite rises slowly as you have reversed the direction it is travelling in. Move back to increase its speed.

Kite turns right

Kite turns right

Kite begins to turn right

Kite turns left

Pull right

Pull right

Pull right

Pull right

1 Steer the kite parallel to the ground. At A, pull sharply with your right hand so the kite does a tight right turn. Bring your hands level so the kite flies straight.

2 At B, pull sharply with your right hand so that the kite turns to your left. Bring your hands level. The kite will fly parallel to the ground.

3 When the kite reaches C, pull right again to make the third corner of the square. Bring your hands level. The kite will rise.

4 At D, do another sharp right turn. Bring your hands level so that the kite flies straight and parallel to the ground again.

MAKING a KITE

Featuring patterns for five different kites, this section shows you step-by-step how to create your own kites. If this is your first attempt at kite-making, start with the sled or Della Porta, then progress on to one of the more complex designs. Choices for materials and equipment are highlighted in a visual glossary. A practical guide to basic techniques ensures a professional finish.

MATERIALS & EQUIPMENT

Most of the materials on these pages are available from specialist kite stores and mail order companies, although mountaineering shops can be a good source of tapes and thick climbing rope. The choice of materials depends on the type of kite you are making. Fiberglass rod, for example, is ideal for the flexible bow of a fighter, although inappropriate for the rigid frame of a box kite, where dowel is best. Kite-making equipment can generally be found around the home; some tools, such as a circle-cutter, give quick, accurate results but are not essential.

TAPES

Ripstop tape
Sticky-backed nylon. Useful for repairs, decoration or reinforcing weak points.

Reinforced tape
A tape with fiberglass strands, which is used to hold spars in place on simple kites and to secure plastic tubing on stunters.

Webbing
Reinforces the noses of stunters. Will also strengthen any other part of a large kite that takes a lot of wear and tear.

Dacron
Sewn on larger stunters to make sleeves for the leading edge spars. Will stand more abrasion than ripstop nylon.

Double-sided tape
Useful for repairs and reinforcement.

Sticky tape
Invaluable for making simple kites, where it is used to stick down spars and strengthen towing points.

FABRICS & THREADS

Ripstop nylon
Lightweight and strong, ripstop is the ideal covering material. It comes in a rainbow of colors.

Plastic
From shopping bags to heavy duty garbage sacks, plastic is a good, cheap covering material for simpler kites.

Mylar
A strong, light, manmade film that has less stretch than plastic. Ideal for simpler kites.

Tyvek
A synthetic material made in the same way as paper, Tyvek does not tear. Not widely available.

Silk
Used to make graceful kites since earliest times. Lightweight and exclusive but expensive and difficult to work.

Paper
From fine tissue to ornate origami papers, paper makes decorative but fragile kites.

Thread
Choose polyester thread as cotton will rot.

LINE

Nylon/polyester line
Cheap and widely available, this is the standard line. It comes smooth or coarse and in a variety of thicknesses and braids.

Thin braided line is ideal for smaller kites

50 lb

100 lb

200 lb

600 lb

650 lb

Braided nylon line | *Thick braided line has a heavier breaking strain than thin; good for larger kites*

50 lb

70 lb

Twisted nylon line | *Twisted line is cheap, although generally braided is best*

100 lb

200 lb

350 lb

Braided polyester line | *Vibrant climbing rope, used for giant kites*

1550 lb

2000 lb

2500 lb

Climbing rope | *Twisted core surrounded by a braided sleeve*

Spectra
Braided from about 1,000 very fine polythene strands, spectra is much thinner and has less stretch than nylon/polyester line. Ideal for performance stunt-flying, where a quick response is essential. Spectra has to be protected with sleeving.

Green and pink spectra are colorful but coarser than white.

Smooth white spectra causes less friction when lines cross during stunting.

Sleeving
Nylon/polyester line from which the core has been removed, sleeving prevents spectra from cutting itself. Spectra is threaded through the sleeve with a special needle.

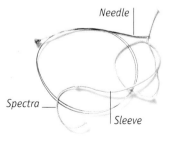

Needle |

Spectra —

Sleeve

Natural line
Not as durable as manmade line and heavier for the same breaking strain.

Glass-coated natural line adds a sharp cutting edge to fighters.

FRAMES & STRUCTURES

Fiberglass
Available as rod or tube. The rod is good for kites that need flex, such as fighters. The tube comes in two varieties: thin wall and thick wall.

.04 in / 1 mm

.08 in / 2 mm

.13 in / 3 mm

.16 in / 4 mm

.19 in / 5 mm

Fiberglass rod

.27 in / 6 mm

.31 in / 8 mm

.43 in / 12 mm

.83 in / 22 mm

Fiberglass tube (thin wall) | *Thin wall is stiffer and lighter*

.29 in / 6.35 mm

.31 in / 8 mm

.43 in / 12 mm

Fiberglass tube (thick wall) | *Thick wall is less likely to break*

Carbon fiber
Stiff and light, carbon fiber is used on many of the latest high-tech stunters as it lasts well under stress.

.24 in / 5.5 mm

.31 in / 8 mm

Dowel
One of the best frame materials, dowel is easy to obtain, light and affordable. Choose ramin dowel or other hardwood varieties.

.13 in / 3 mm

.16 in / 4 mm

.27 in / 6 mm

.31 in / 8 mm

.43 in / 12 mm

.58 in / 15 mm

Bamboo
Like silk, a traditional material. The very thick stems are split down to size.

Piece of split bamboo

RINGS & SWIVELS

O rings

D rings

Split rings

Aluminum rings
An O ring is tied to the bridle and the line attached. A D ring is sewn in with a tab. Split rings are used on some box kites.

This part clips on to a ring on the kite

The line is tied on to the bottom loop

Standard swivels, for small to medium-sized kites and drogues.

Deep sea fishing swivel, good for large kites and spinning drogues.

Large fishing swivel

Swivel clips
An easy way to attach the flying line or a drogue to the kite. The clips rotate so line does not twist when wound in.

JOINTS

Ferruling
Tubing for joining spars in a straight line. Usually made from aluminum and cut to size.

The cross-spar slots in at each end

Dihedral pieces
V-shaped pieces keep the kite face at a constant angle.

OTHER ACCESSORIES

Sliders
Aluminum sliders help bow the cross-spar. The slider is threaded on to the line attached to the spar, and moved along the line to bow the spar.

End caps
Made from rubber, these are put on the ends of some spars to stop their abrasive edges rubbing against pockets and wearing through them.

Notches
These can be slotted on to the ends of a manmade spar, enabling it to house line.

Plastic tubing
Cut to an angle, this is used to join cross-spars to leading edge spars on stunters (see page 65).

Fluorescent beads are for night-flying

Beads
Strung on line attached to a tab on the cover, these tiny plastic beads are used to adjust tension on box kites. They slot behind the notch on a spar; the more beads behind the notch, the greater the tension.

EQUIPMENT

MARKING & MEASURING

Tailor's chalk
For marking out the cutting pattern on the fabric.

Felt-tip pen
An alternative to tailor's chalk. Choose a pen with a fine tip.

Card template for a sled

Template
Usually a plate or a cut-out shape from card, a template saves time when making more than one simple kite or cutting vents in the cover.

Ruler/set square
For transcribing the cutting pattern on to the fabric. It is important to be precise.

CUTTING

Scissors
Use sharp scissors for cutting fabric. Keep a pair specially for this purpose.

Circle cutter
Similar to a pair of compasses with a blade instead of a pencil, a circle cutter makes neat vents in ripstop nylon or plastic.

Soldering iron
Cutting nylon with a soldering iron seals the edges and stops them fraying. For speed, choose one with a rating of 30-40 W. A soldering iron can also be used for heat-sealing line.

Rotary cutter
A knife with a very fine rotating round blade for cutting ripstop nylon. Best used with a template.

Modelling knife
Used mainly to cut plastic, mylar and paper, as it can pull nylon.

OTHER EQUIPMENT

Hacksaw
Use a small hacksaw for cutting lengths of dowel and notches in the ends.

File
A small wood file is best for rounding the ends of dowel.

Lighter or matches
For heat-sealing the ends of line.

Wide-eyed needle
For threading line through tabs and the cover.

TECHNIQUES
See pages 64-5

Cutting

Heat-sealing

Preparing dowel

USEFUL TECHNIQUES

The practical techniques on these pages are essential for kite-making, enabling you to achieve truly professional results. Detailed steps demonstrate simple but effective methods for attaching spars to the cover, tying on a bridle, preparing dowel, heat-sealing line and cutting fabric. Pockets, tabs and reinforcing patches are easily made from scrap nylon; for speed, sew more than one tab or patch at a time. On larger kites, the fabric around the pocket or tab may need strengthening with extra layers of nylon.

MAKING A POCKET

A small fabric envelope, sewn to the cover at an angle, a pocket holds the end of a spar.

Nylon strip

Folded strip

1 Cut a strip of ripstop nylon, 7 in (18 cm) long and 1 in (2.5 cm) wide. Fold the strip over so that it is half its original length and repeat.

2 Pin the folded strip at a 45° angle to the kite edge, overlapping it by nearly half the length of the strip. Sew the strip to the kite across the corner of the kite.

The pocket should slightly overhang the kite edge

3 Fold in the longer end to create a pocket. Sew along the pocket sides to seal them.

MAKING TABS

Tabs are short strips of fabric, doubled over and sewn to the cover to house line.

1 Cut a strip of nylon 1 in (2.5 cm) wide; allow 2 in (5 cm) in length for each tab.

Sides folded and partly sewn

Sewn strip

2 in lengths

2 Fold in the two long sides so that the strip is a third of its original width. Sew the strip down the center over the folded sides, and cut into 2 in (5 cm) lengths.

MAKING REINFORCING PATCHES

These triangular patches strengthen a hole so that it does not give when you insert a spar. Stick the patch down first, then cut the hole.

Tape stuck on nylon

Nylon-backed tape

1 Cut a length of double-sided carpet tape, allowing 2 in (5 cm) for each pair of patches, and stick it to a scrap of nylon. Trim the nylon around the tape.

2 in length

Triangular patches

Hole cut in reinforcing patch

Patch stuck in place

2 Cut the tape into 2 in (5 cm) lengths and cut each length in half diagonally. Peel off the backing and stick the patch in position on the kite. Cut a hole in the patch (see below) to insert the spar.

CUTTING A HOLE

It is best to use a circle cutter to cut a hole, although you can draw the circle with a pair of compasses and cut it out with scissors, or even use a soldering iron and template. Put the point of the cutter in the center of where you want the hole to be, adjust the cutter to the right diameter, then cut the hole.

HOT-CUTTING FABRIC

Use a soldering iron to hot-cut nylon or webbing and stop the edges from fraying. When the iron has heated up, hold the handle like a pen and carefully trace the point along a straight edge or template.

WARNINGS
▲ When hot-cutting, make sure that the room is well ventilated as the material gives off fumes.
▲ Take care not to burn your fingers when heat-sealing line.

HEAT-SEALING LINE
Use matches, a lighter or a soldering iron to melt the ends of line and stop them fraying.

PREPARING DOWEL

1 Cut the dowel to length with a small hacksaw and use a file to round the ends.

---

2 If you need to make a notch in the ends to house loops of line, saw to a depth of ¼ in (5 mm) halfway across each end.

JOINING SPARS AT AN ANGLE

1 Cut a piece of plastic tube 1¼-3 in (3-8 cm) long, depending on the diameter of the spar, and midway along cut a slot with a pair of scissors halfway across its width.

2 Make another cut at a 45° angle to the first to create a wedge shape. Bend the tube down at the wedge to angle it and insert the spars.

Fitting the spars

The cross-spar slots into here

The leading edge spar passes through here

TYING KNOTS

These are the basic knots in kite-making. The overhand and slip knots are mainly used in constructing a kite. The lark's head knot attaches the ring to the bridle and is easily moved to adjust the flight angle. The bowline knot is good for tying the flying line to the bridle ring.

OVERHAND KNOT

1   2   3

SLIP KNOT

1   2   3

BOWLINE KNOT

1   2   3

LARK'S HEAD KNOT

1   2   3

SIMPLE SLED

One of the easiest kites to make, this sled involves little more than hemming the nylon, sewing sleeves to hold the spars on each side and hot-cutting two vents. Designed for light to moderate winds, the kite is flown on line with a breaking strain of 50-70 lb (25-32 kg). If the sled does not fly perfectly straight, move the bridle ring away from the direction the kite favors.

MATERIALS & EQUIPMENT

- ▲ 3 ft (1 m) ripstop nylon
- ▲ 8 ft (2.5 m) of 50 lb (25 kg) braided nylon line
- ▲ One aluminum ring
- ▲ Two 35 in (88 cm) lengths of 1/4 in (6 mm) ramin dowel
- ▲ Flying line

- ▲ Pen or tailor's chalk
- ▲ Ruler/set square
- ▲ Scissors
- ▲ Pins
- ▲ Sewing machine and thread
- ▲ Matches or lighter
- ▲ Soldering iron
- ▲ Plate (diameter approx. 7 in [18 cm])
- ▲ File

Dowel *Ring*

Ripstop nylon *Line*

1 Following the cutting pattern, mark and cut out the ripstop nylon.

21¼ in
10 in
28¼ in

1¼ in   18¾ in   ½ in hem

Sleeve line

2 Fold over, pin and sew a ½ in (1 cm) hem around the edge of the cover. Draw the sleeve lines and turn the fabric over so that the lines face down.

COLORWAYS

Fin folded over

Seam

½ in gap

3 Fold over a fin so that the sleeve lines are together. Seam the sleeve, sewing across both ends and leaving a ½ in (1 cm) gap, ½ in (1 cm) from the bottom. Repeat with the other fin.

The doubled-over tab sits either side of the point

4 Make two tabs from scrap ripstop nylon and stitch to the points of the fins.

The legs of the bridle should be the same length

5 Heat-seal the ends of the line. Tie one end to each tab and using a lark's head knot, attach the ring at the line midpoint.

6 Using a soldering iron and the plate as a template, hot-cut two circles 6 in (15 cm) from the bottom of the kite. These form the vents.

7 Round the ends of the dowel and insert each length into a sleeve through a gap. The spars should fit tightly without distortion. Tie the flying line to the ring.

Shaped by the wind
In flight, the wind billows out the cover and gives it a curved shape. The vents add stability.

TECHNIQUES
See pages 64-5

Making tabs

Heat-sealing

Lark's head knot

Hot-cutting

Preparing dowel

DELLA PORTA

Basically just a rectangle of fabric with two diagonal spars, four pockets and a long loop tail, the classic Della Porta is simple to make. To vary the look, appliqué the cover or make it from bands of different-colored ripstop nylon sewn together. The kite is very stable in a wide range of winds. It should be flown on line with a breaking strain of 25 lb (12 kg).

MATERIALS & EQUIPMENT

▲ 3³/₄ ft (1.15 m) ripstop nylon
▲ Two 31¹/₂ in (80 cm) lengths of ¹/₄ in (6 mm) ramin dowel
▲ About 7 ft (2.2 m) of 50 lb (25 kg) braided nylon line
▲ One aluminum ring
▲ Flying line

▲ Pen or tailor's chalk
▲ Ruler/set square
▲ Scissors
▲ Pins
▲ Sewing machine and thread
▲ File
▲ Matches or lighter
▲ Wide-eyed needle

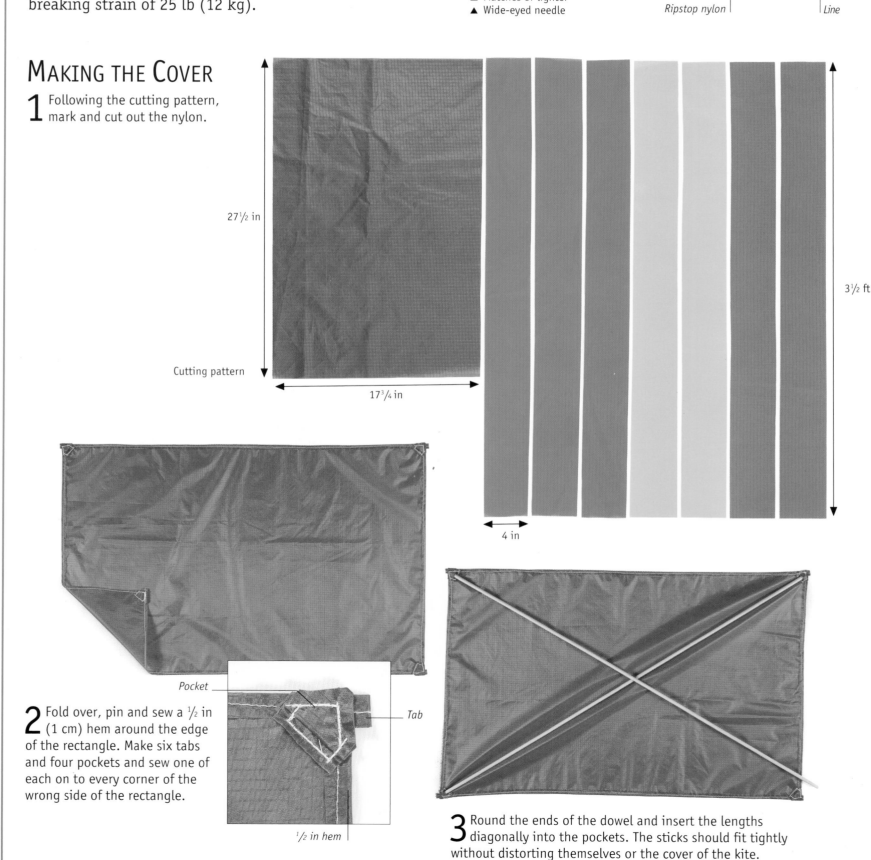

Dowel *Ring*

Ripstop nylon *Line*

MAKING THE COVER

1 Following the cutting pattern, mark and cut out the nylon.

27¹/₂ in

Cutting pattern

17³/₄ in

3¹/₂ ft

4 in

2 Fold over, pin and sew a ¹/₂ in (1 cm) hem around the edge of the rectangle. Make six tabs and four pockets and sew one of each on to every corner of the wrong side of the rectangle.

Pocket

Tab

¹/₂ in hem

3 Round the ends of the dowel and insert the lengths diagonally into the pockets. The sticks should fit tightly without distorting themselves or the cover of the kite.

ATTACHING THE BRIDLE

The legs of the bridle should be the same length

Center loop securing the sticks

1 Cut the line into a 3 ft (1 m) length, a 24½ in (62 cm) length and three 6 in (15 cm) lengths, and heat-seal the ends. Tie the ring with a lark's head knot halfway along the 3 ft (1 m) length, then tie each end to the tabs at the top corners of the kite.

2 Use a wide-eyed needle to thread a 6 in (15 cm) length through to the front of the kite on one side of the crossed sticks. Bring the length up again to the back on the other side of the sticks. Tie an overhand knot to create a small loop.

3 Pull the loop through to the front and using slip knots, tie one end of the 24½ in (62 cm) length to the center loop and the other end to the ring. Tie the flying line to the ring.

ADDING A TAIL

Slit

Seam joining two strips

1 Sew the strips of ripstop together end to end to make a tail, and cut slits randomly in both sides.

The doubled-over tab sits either side of the nylon

2 Sew a tab to each tail end. Thread a 6 in (15 cm) length of line through each tab, line up the ends and tie an overhand knot near the tab. Tie the tail to the tabs at the bottom corners.

Stable in flight
Once the kite is airborne, the long loop tail keeps it on a straight course if it wanders to one side.

TECHNIQUES
See pages 64-5

Making tabs

Making a pocket

Preparing dowel

Heat-sealing

Lark's head knot

Overhand knot

Slip knot

SIX-PACK

A six-celled soft kite based on the sled design, the Six-pack flies at a very high angle and in a wide range of winds. It is fairly simple to make because of its lack of spars and needs no assembly. The fins on the cover are a contrasting color; for a different effect, add a third color into the design, or make a kite of one color. The Six-pack should be flown with a drogue and on line with a breaking strain of 25-50 lb (12-25 kg).

MATERIALS & EQUIPMENT

▲ 6½ ft (2 m) ripstop nylon
▲ 40 ft (12 m) of 50 lb (25 kg) braided nylon line
▲ Two aluminum rings
▲ One swivel clip

▲ Pen or tailor's chalk
▲ Ruler/set square
▲ Scissors
▲ Sewing machine and thread
▲ Pins
▲ Matches or lighter
▲ Wide-eyed needle

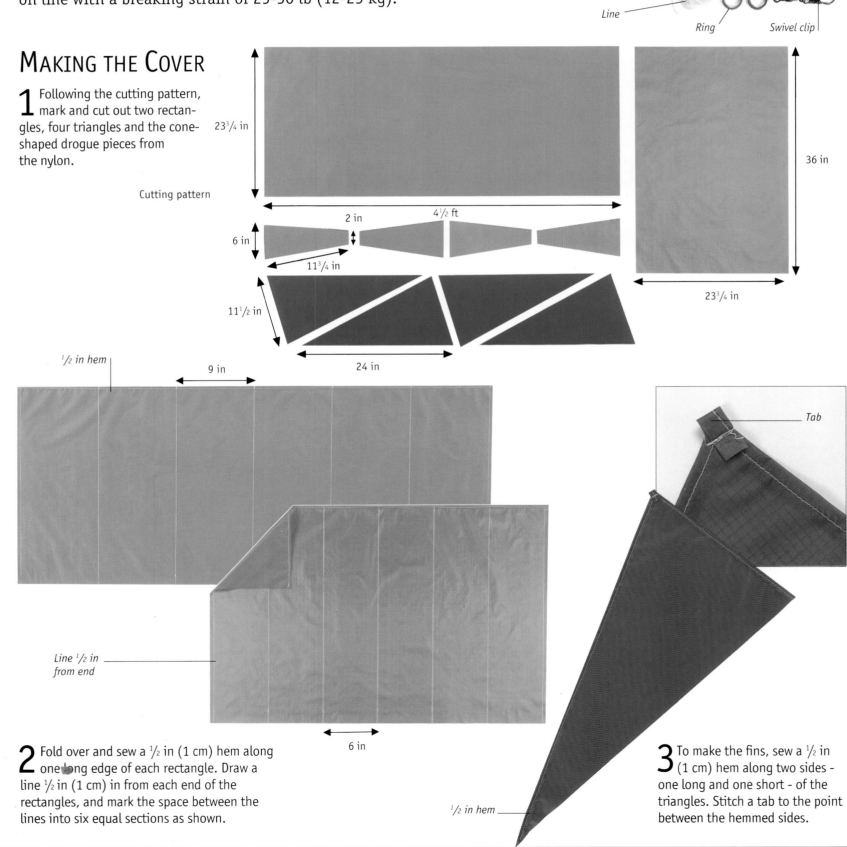

Ripstop nylon

Line

Ring

Swivel clip

MAKING THE COVER

1 Following the cutting pattern, mark and cut out two rectangles, four triangles and the cone-shaped drogue pieces from the nylon.

Cutting pattern

23¾ in

2 in

4½ ft

6 in

11¾ in

11½ in

24 in

36 in

23¾ in

½ in hem

9 in

Line ½ in from end

6 in

Tab

½ in hem

2 Fold over and sew a ½ in (1 cm) hem along one long edge of each rectangle. Draw a line ½ in (1 cm) in from each end of the rectangles, and mark the space between the lines into six equal sections as shown.

3 To make the fins, sew a ½ in (1 cm) hem along two sides - one long and one short - of the triangles. Stitch a tab to the point between the hemmed sides.

Fin between pieces of fabric

Seam ½ in from edge

4 Place the rectangles with right sides facing and one end of each together. Put a fin between the two and pin. Sew ½ in (1 cm) in from the edge.

5 Repeat with the other end, aligning the edges of the rectangles and sewing another fin between the two.

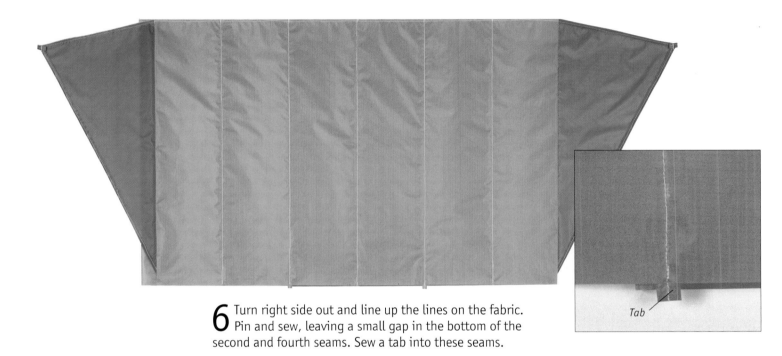

Tab

6 Turn right side out and line up the lines on the fabric. Pin and sew, leaving a small gap in the bottom of the second and fourth seams. Sew a tab into these seams.

Cell

Sew up 2 in

7 Pin the two remaining fins to the kite face over the second and fourth seams, and sew in place. At the bottom of the kite, pin the midpoint of the front and back of each cell together. Sew up 2 in (5 cm).

TECHNIQUES
See pages 64-5

Making tabs

Heat-sealing

Overhand knot

Lark's head knot

ATTACHING THE BRIDLE

1 Cut two 10 ft (3 m) lengths of 50 lb (25 kg) line and heat-seal the ends. Thread the lengths through a ring and line up the ends. Tie an overhand knot near the ring. Then, tie one end to each fin tab.

2 Cut a 20 in (50 cm) length of 50 lb (25 kg) line and heat-seal the ends. Tie one end to each tab at the bottom of the kite. Using a lark's head knot, tie the other ring at the midpoint of this line.

ADDING A DROGUE

½ in hem

Seam joining two drogue pieces

1 Sew the drogue pieces together, then fold over and sew a ½ in (1 cm) hem around the top (the wider part). With the seams outside, sew the last two sides together to make a tube. Turn right side out.

Make sure that the lines are the same length

2 Cut two 20 in (50 cm) lengths of 50 lb (25 kg) line and heat-seal the ends. Thread the lengths through the loop on the bottom of the swivel clip and line up the ends. Tie an overhand knot near the loop. Use a needle to thread one end through the top of a seam joining two drogue pieces and tie off. Repeat with the other ends.

3 Take the last length of 50 lb (25 kg) line and tie one end to the ring on the bottom of the kite. Tie an overhand knot to create a loop in the other end, and clip on the drogue. Tie the flying line to the bridle ring.

A soft kite
The Six-Pack is inflated by the wind through the open leading edge and makes a dramatic sight in the sky.

TUMBLING STAR

A multi-faceted, single-celled box kite, the Tumbling Star is great fun to fly as it rolls and tumbles in light to moderate winds. Making the six-pointed Star is not as complicated as it looks because many of the steps are repetitive. Choose different colors of ripstop nylon for the central section and the points on the Star so that they alternate as the kite tumbles. Fly the Star on line with a breaking strain of 50 lb (25 kg).

MATERIALS & EQUIPMENT

▲ 5¼ ft (1.6 m) ripstop nylon
▲ 8 ft (2.5 m) of 50 lb (25 kg) braided nylon line
▲ Six 11½ in (29 cm) lengths of ¼ in (6 mm) ramin dowel
▲ Three 3½ ft (1.05 m) lengths of ¼ in (6 mm) ramin dowel
▲ One aluminum ring
▲ Flying line

▲ Pen or tailor's chalk
▲ Ruler/set square
▲ Scissors
▲ Sewing machine and thread
▲ Circle cutter
▲ Pins
▲ Matches or lighter
▲ File
▲ Hacksaw

Dowel
Ripstop nylon
Line   *Ring*

MAKING THE CENTRAL SECTION

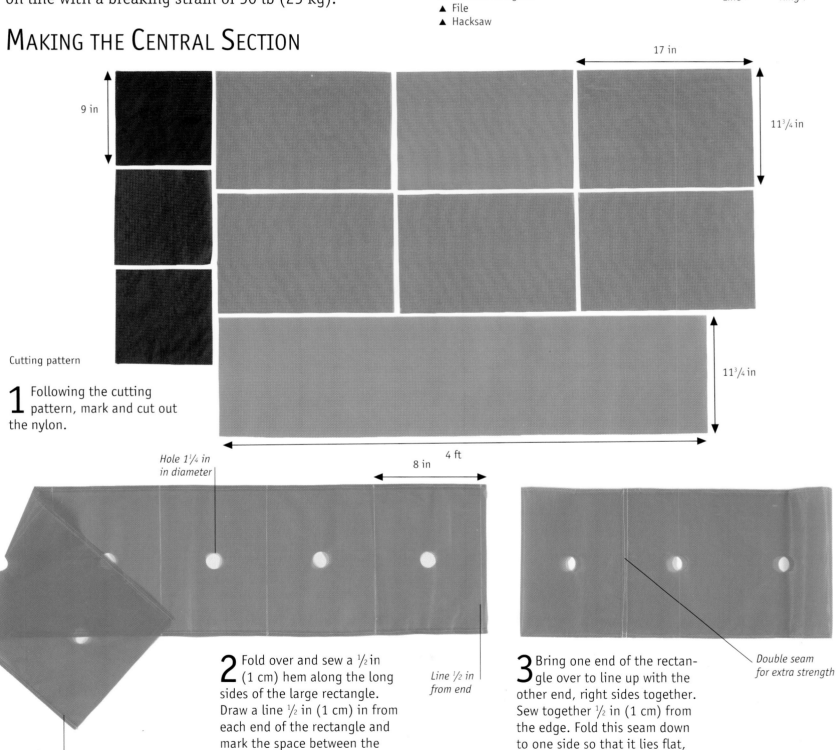

9 in

17 in

11³/₄ in

11³/₄ in

Cutting pattern

1 Following the cutting pattern, mark and cut out the nylon.

4 ft

8 in

Hole 1¼ in in diameter

½ in hem

2 Fold over and sew a ½ in (1 cm) hem along the long sides of the large rectangle. Draw a line ½ in (1 cm) in from each end of the rectangle and mark the space between the lines into six equal sections. Cut a circular hole in the center of each section.

Line ½ in from end

3 Bring one end of the rectangle over to line up with the other end, right sides together. Sew together ½ in (1 cm) from the edge. Fold this seam down to one side so that it lies flat, and sew. Turn right side out.

Double seam for extra strength

73

ADDING THE POINTS

½ in hem

8½ in

Right side of fabric

1 To make the outer panels, sew a ½ in (1 cm) hem along the long sides of each small rectangle. Mark into two equal sections.

2 Join the panels to the central section, aligning the line on each panel with a section line. Pin and sew.

½ in gap

Seam

3 Pin the end of one panel to the end of the next. Sew ¾ in (2 cm) in from the edge, leaving a ½ in (1 cm) gap in the seam at one end. Repeat with the other panels.

MAKING THE WINGS

½ in hem

The doubled-over tab sits either side of the corner

Make all the loops the same size

Sew across here

Sleeve

1 Fold over, pin and sew a ½ in (1 cm) hem around the edge of each square. Make nine tabs and stitch a tab to two opposite corners of the squares.

2 Cut six 4 in (10 cm) lengths of 50 lb (25 kg) line and heat-seal the ends. Thread a length through a tab and tie an overhand knot to make a loop. Repeat with the other lengths. Cut the squares in half diagonally to create two triangles.

3 Put a wing between the flaps where the end of one panel meets another. Pin across the top of the flaps, and sew. Then sew down the ends of the flaps to make an enclosed sleeve.

Hole 1¼ in in diameter

The end with the tabs becomes the front

4 Repeat with the other wings, making sure that they all face the same way, sewing a tab into the same end of every other sleeve, as you seal the ends.

5 Stick a reinforcing patch below a sleeve halfway across the same side of each point. Cut holes through the patches.

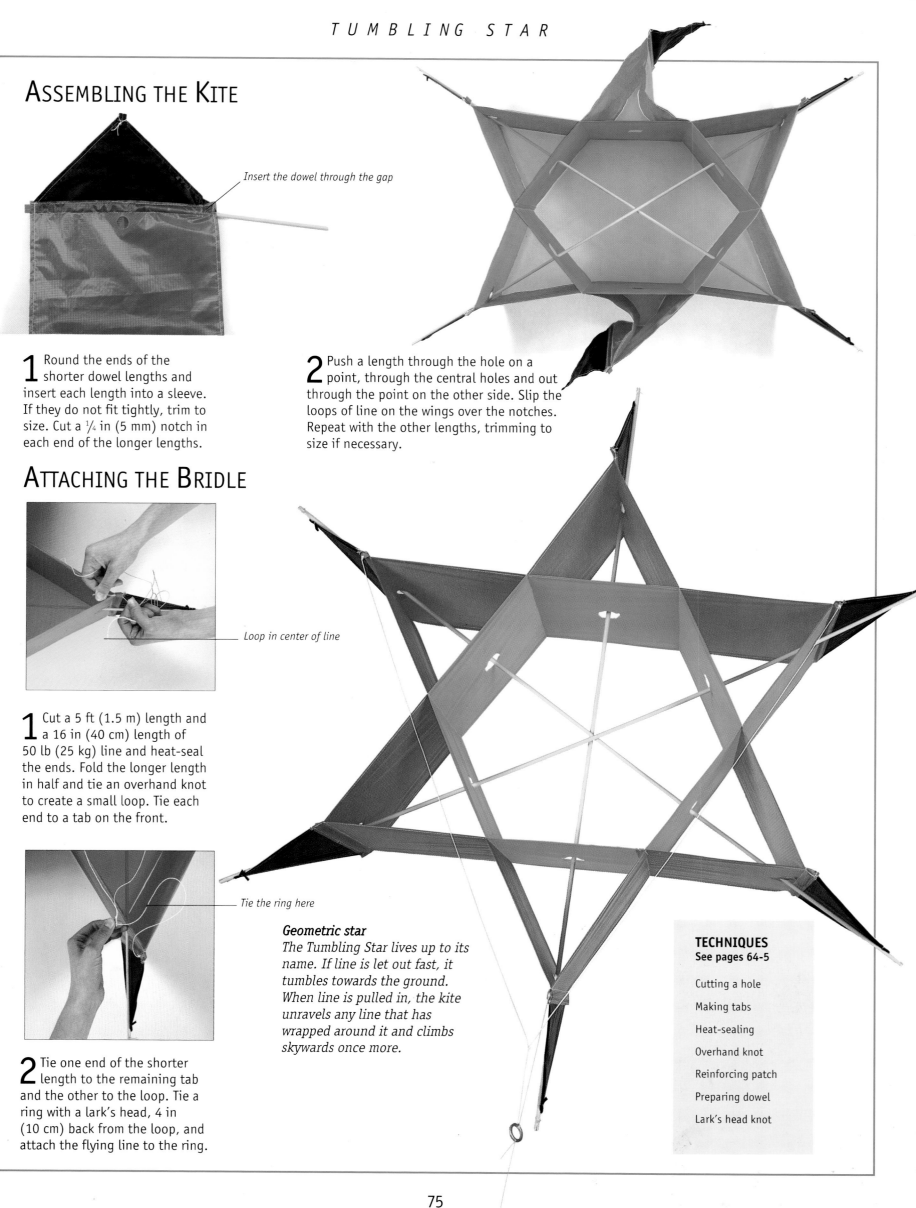

ASSEMBLING THE KITE

Insert the dowel through the gap

1 Round the ends of the shorter dowel lengths and insert each length into a sleeve. If they do not fit tightly, trim to size. Cut a ¼ in (5 mm) notch in each end of the longer lengths.

2 Push a length through the hole on a point, through the central holes and out through the point on the other side. Slip the loops of line on the wings over the notches. Repeat with the other lengths, trimming to size if necessary.

ATTACHING THE BRIDLE

Loop in center of line

1 Cut a 5 ft (1.5 m) length and a 16 in (40 cm) length of 50 lb (25 kg) line and heat-seal the ends. Fold the longer length in half and tie an overhand knot to create a small loop. Tie each end to a tab on the front.

Tie the ring here

2 Tie one end of the shorter length to the remaining tab and the other to the loop. Tie a ring with a lark's head, 4 in (10 cm) back from the loop, and attach the flying line to the ring.

Geometric star
The Tumbling Star lives up to its name. If line is let out fast, it tumbles towards the ground. When line is pulled in, the kite unravels any line that has wrapped around it and climbs skywards once more.

TECHNIQUES
See pages 64-5

Cutting a hole

Making tabs

Heat-sealing

Overhand knot

Reinforcing patch

Preparing dowel

Lark's head knot

STUNTER

This highly maneuverable stunt kite combines a streamlined delta shape with the simple construction of a fighter. Made in two halves, which are then joined together, the stunter has only a flexible bow and a spine for its framework. Once airborne, the kite can perform all the basic stunt maneuvers, from looping the loop to describing squares and figures of eight. Fly the stunter on line with a breaking strain of 40 lb (18 kg).

MATERIALS & EQUIPMENT

▲ 31½ in (80 cm) ripstop nylon
▲ One 23 in (58 cm) length and one 5½ ft (1.7 m) length of ¼ in (4 mm) fiberglass rod
▲ About 6 ft (1.9 m) of 50 lb (25 kg) braided nylon line
▲ Two aluminum rings
▲ Two 100 ft (30 m) lengths of flying line

▲ Pen or tailor's chalk
▲ Ruler/set square
▲ Scissors
▲ Sewing machine and thread
▲ Matches or lighter
▲ Wide-eyed needle

Nylon

Rod   Line   Ring

MAKING THE COVER

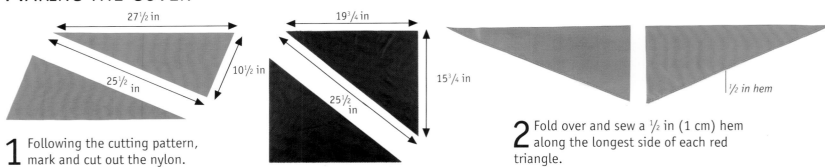

27½ in

25½ in

10½ in

19¾ in

25½ in

15¾ in

½ in hem

1 Following the cutting pattern, mark and cut out the nylon.

2 Fold over and sew a ½ in (1 cm) hem along the longest side of each red triangle.

3 Sew a red triangle to a black triangle as shown, allowing a ½ in (1 cm) seam. Repeat with the other triangles, reversing the way that they face.

½ in seam

Each pair of triangles forms half of the kite

4 Open out one pair of triangles so that the seam faces up and fold it over on to the black triangle. Sew down the seam and continue to sew along the edge of the triangle to hem it. Repeat with the other triangles.

Double seam for extra strength

½ in hem

2 in gap

Wing

10 in

Sew along the bottom of the pointed tip

5 To make a sleeve to hold the bow, mark a line, 1½ in (4 cm) in from the straight edge formed by the two triangles. Fold the edge over to align with the line. Sew close to the edge, leaving a 2 in (5 cm) gap in the hem as shown. Seal the sleeve by sewing along the wingtip. Repeat with the other pair of triangles.

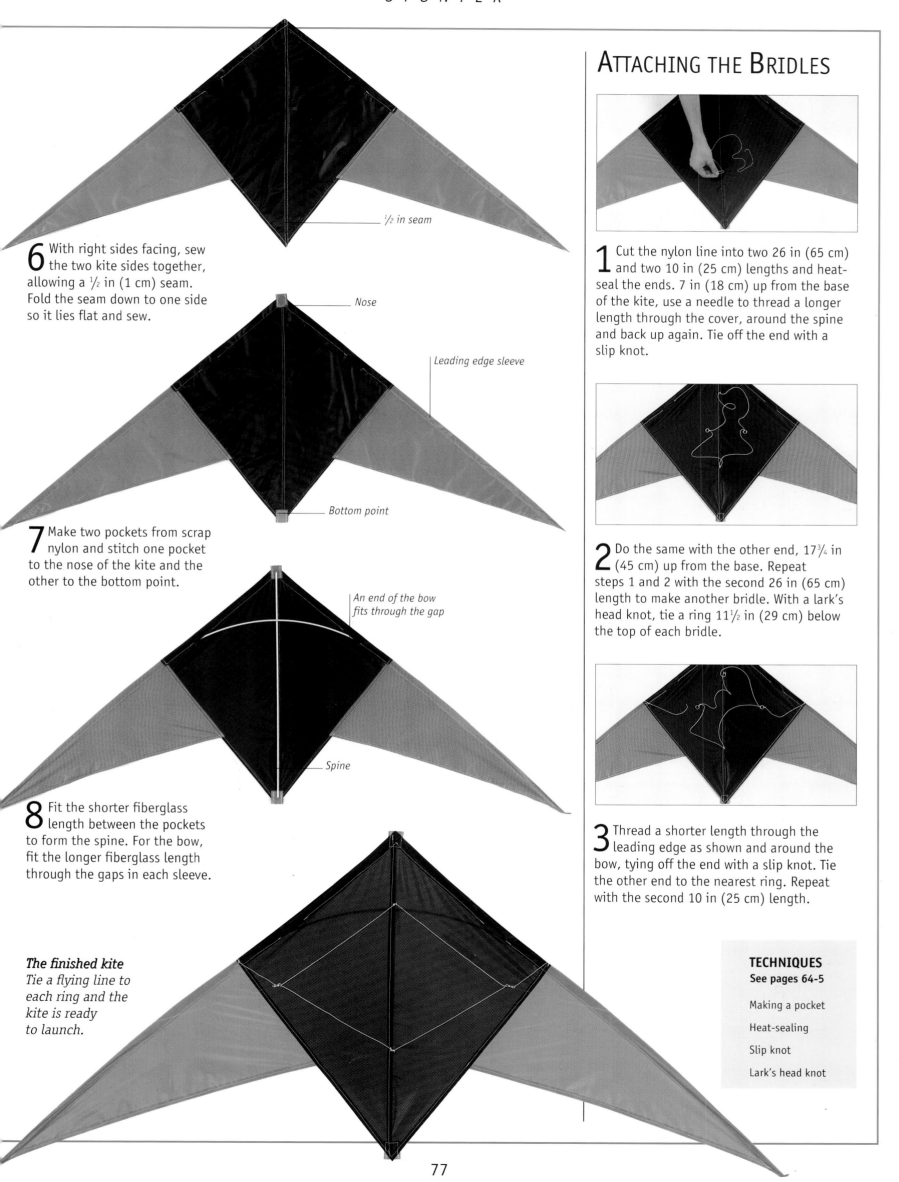

6 With right sides facing, sew the two kite sides together, allowing a ½ in (1 cm) seam. Fold the seam down to one side so it lies flat and sew.

½ in seam

7 Make two pockets from scrap nylon and stitch one pocket to the nose of the kite and the other to the bottom point.

Nose

Leading edge sleeve

Bottom point

8 Fit the shorter fiberglass length between the pockets to form the spine. For the bow, fit the longer fiberglass length through the gaps in each sleeve.

An end of the bow fits through the gap

Spine

The finished kite
Tie a flying line to each ring and the kite is ready to launch.

ATTACHING THE BRIDLES

1 Cut the nylon line into two 26 in (65 cm) and two 10 in (25 cm) lengths and heat-seal the ends. 7 in (18 cm) up from the base of the kite, use a needle to thread a longer length through the cover, around the spine and back up again. Tie off the end with a slip knot.

2 Do the same with the other end, 17¾ in (45 cm) up from the base. Repeat steps 1 and 2 with the second 26 in (65 cm) length to make another bridle. With a lark's head knot, tie a ring 11½ in (29 cm) below the top of each bridle.

3 Thread a shorter length through the leading edge as shown and around the bow, tying off the end with a slip knot. Tie the other end to the nearest ring. Repeat with the second 10 in (25 cm) length.

TECHNIQUES
See pages 64-5

Making a pocket

Heat-sealing

Slip knot

Lark's head knot

SUPPLIERS & ORGANIZATIONS

ALASKA

FLIGHTS OF FANCY, University Center, 3901 Old Seward Hwy #12E, Anchorage, AK 99503 907-563-5483

ARIZONA

THE KITE CORNER inside the Firehouse, 520 W. Sheldon, #4, Prescott, AZ 86301 602-445-2344

ARKANSAS

KALEIDOKITES, 1C Spring Street, Eureka Springs, AR 72632 501-253-6596

CALIFORNIA

ALL ABOUT KITES, 3689 B Midway Dr., San Diego, CA 92110 619-224-1610

BAY BREEZE, 129-C First St., Tannery Bldg., Benecia, CA 94510 707-747-9403

CALIFORNIA KITE OUTLET, 332 Mississippi St., San Francisco, CA 94107

COME FLY A KITE, 1228 State St., Santa Barbara, CA 93101 805-966-2694

CANDY & KITES, 1415 Highway 1, Bodega Bay, CA 94923 707-875-3777

KALEIDOSCOPE KITES, 517 Ocean Front Walk, #19 Venice, CA 90291 213-396-9699

KITE EMPORIUM, 150 Hinds St, Pismo Beach, CA 93449

LET'S FLY A KITE, 13755 Fiji Way, Marina Del Rey, CA 90292 213-822-2561

RENEGADE KITES, 3769 Peralta Blvd., Fremont, CA 94536 415-791-5666

COLORADO

INTO THE WIND, 1408 Peral St, Boulder, CO 80302 800-541-0314

CONNECTICUT

ALL WIND SPORTS, 80 Pane Road, Newington, CT 06111 203-667-1457

DELAWARE

AIR TRAFFIC, Garfield Parkway, Bethany Beach, DE 19930 302-539-5411

DISTRICT OF COLUMBIA

KITE LOFT OF NATIONAL PLACE, 1331 Pennsylvania Ave., NW 227, Washington DC, 20004

FLORIDA

GIFT OF WINGS, Marriott Hotel, 100 N. Atlantic Ave., Daytona Beach, FL 32108 904-257-1599

KITERIGGERS, 420 Wharfside Way, Jacksonville, FL 32207 904-399-KITE

GEORGIA

SAVANNAH SAILS & RAILS, 423 E. River St., Savannah, GA 31401 912-232-7201

HAWAII

BIG WIND KITE FACTORY, 120 Maunaloa Hwy., Maunaloa, Molokai, HI 96770 808-552-2364

ILLINOIS

CHICAGO KITE CO., 5065 Dukes Berry Ln., Barrington, IL 60010 708-359-2556

IOWA

SODBUSTER'S SKY TOYS, 105 S. Polk, Pleasantville, IA 50225 515-848-5686

KANSAS

AIR ADVENTURES, 3101 N. Rock Rd., Ste. 105, Wichita, KS 67226 316-634-1772

LOUISIANA

THE KITE CONNECTION, 107 Funderburk, Houma, LA 70364 504-851-4287

MAINE

FREE AS THE BREEZE, 134 Front St., Bath, ME 04530 207-443-2213

MARYLAND

THE KITE LOFT, Harborplace, Baltimore, MD 301-528-0888

MASSACHUSETTS

FLY BY NIGHT KITES, 294 Court St., Rte. 3A, Plymouth, MA 02360 503-746-0555

KITES OF BOSTON, Second Floor Core, North Market Building, Boston, MA 02109 617-742-1455

MICHIGAN

GRAND BAY KITE COMPANY, 121 E. Front St., Traverse City, MI 49684 616-929-0607

MISSISSIPPI

WIND VENTURES KITE SHOP, Edgewater Mall, 2600 Beach Blvd., Biloxi, MS 39531 601-388-9463

NEVADA

KITE PIT, 3502 S. Virginia, Suite 115, BayA6, Reno, NV 89509 702-829-7404

NEW HAMPSHIRE

KITES, 60 Silver Lake, Marlborough, NH 03455 608-827-3014

NEW JERSEY

1900 KITES & BIKES, 1922 Boardwalk, N. Wildwood, NJ 08260 609-729-7329

NEW YORK

BIG CITY KITES, 1201 Lexington Ave., New York, NY 10028 212-472-2623

KITE WORLD, 353 Harry L. Dr., Johnson City, NY 13790 607-729-5700

KITES OF THE HARBOUR, Main St., Sag Harbor, NY 11963

NORTH CAROLINA

KITE MASTERS, 351 S. College Road, #23 Wilmington, NC 28403 919-452-4456

OHIO

ON THE WIND, Heritage Square, Grand Rapids, OH 43522 419-832-KITE

OKLAHOMA

KINETIC KITES, 6313 Willowridge Dr., Bethany, OK 405-722-KITE

OREGON

CATCH THE WIND, 266 S.E. Highway 101, Lincoln City, OR 97367 800-227-7878

PENNSYLVANIA

THE FAMILY KITE, Harrisburg City Island, Harrisburg, PA 717-232-7650

RHODE ISLAND

AIRBORNE KITES, Bannisters Wharf, Newport, RI 22840 401-849-5688

SOUTH CAROLINA

KITES FLY'N HIGH, The Rainbow Market, 40 N. Market St., Charleston SC 29401 803-577-3529

TEXAS

KITES UNLIMITED, Houston, TX , 713-589-6272

UTAH

AIR APPARENT KITES, 396 Trolley Square, Salt Lake City, UT, 84102 801-531-7434

VIRGINIA

KITE KOOP, Landmark Plaza, Chincoteague, VA 23336 804-336-5554

WASHINGTON

CITY KITES, 1501 Western Ave., Seattle, WA 98101 206-622-5349

WISCONSIN

FISH CREEK KITE COMPANY, 3853 Highway 42, Fish Creek, WI 54212 414-868-3769

ACKNOWLEDGMENTS

Authors' acknowledgments: We would like to thank the following people for their invaluable help during the writing of this book: Andy King and Viv Walters from the Kite Store for lending kites for photoshoots and giving us support, Sarah Kent for her input and modelling in the Flying Kites section, Gill and Jon Bloom for going over final text, and Tim Walker for photographing us at short notice.

Thanks to our editor, Tanya Hines, whose skill and tireless efforts have brought the whole book together, and Daphne Razazan for her guidance, especially during the early stages of the project. To Nigel Osborne and Matthew Chattle for their design and photographic skills.

We are grateful to the following for the use of their kites: The Kite Store, Martin Lester, Windy Kites, Joel Scholz, High Flyers, Peter Lynn, Top of the Line, Tony Slater, Raindrop Kites, Graham Wyle, Wolfgang Schimmelpfennig, Rare Air Kites, John Barker (parachuting teddy).

Dorling Kindersley would like to thank The Kite Store for loaning kites for photography, Sarah Kent for her expertise and modelling in the book, Gill and Jon Bloom for checking proofs, and Andy Smith for help on the aerodynamics section. Thanks also to Mark Thomson for computer page layouts and Hilary Bird for the index.

Photographic credits
All photographs by Matthew Chattle except:
Barnaby's Picture Library, Robin Dawson: p.1; Gill and Jon Bloom: pp.8-9; Paul Bricknell: pp.34, 36c, 36-7 (main pic); Martin Cameron: pp.44, 45 (all pix except tl & box kite), 46-7 (main pic); Sarah Kent: pp.17bl, 35tr, 46t; Pictor International: pp.42-3; Susanna Price: pp.14t, 21tr, 24 (boxed pic), 32l, 33, 37tr, 43 (inset), 46b, 59 (inset); Anne Ronan Picture Library: pp.10, 11tl; Royal Aeronautical Society: p.11tr; Tim Walker: p.6
Key: t = top; b = bottom; c = center; l = left; r = right